Downeast

Downeast

Five Maine Girls and the
Unseen Story of Rural America

Gigi Georges

HARPER
An Imprint of HarperCollins*Publishers*

HarperCollins books may be purchased for educational, business, or sales promotional use. For information, please email the Special Markets Department at SPsales@harpercollins.com.

FIRST EDITION

Designed by Leah Carlson-Stanisic

Illustrations © Арина Трапезникова / stock.adobe.com

Library of Congress Cataloging-in-Publication Data has been applied for.

ISBN 978-0-06-298445-6

21 22 23 24 25   LSC   10 9 8 7 6 5 4 3 2 1

To Margaux and Chris
My Angels, on Earth and in Heaven

Author's Note

This is a work of nonfiction. The events described were directly witnessed by me, or were relayed to me by members of the Downeast Washington County community between 2016 and 2020. Interviews were digitally recorded or documented through text messages or email exchanges. The names of the girls featured in this work—as well as their relatives, friends, teachers, mentors, places of worship, local businesses, and some addresses—have been changed to protect their privacy. However, the names of the towns, high school and other local institutions, boats, and key geographical markers have not been altered.

We shall not cease from exploration

And the end of all our exploring

Will be to arrive where we started

And know the place for the first time.

—T. S. Eliot, *Little Gidding*

Contents

Part Four: **The Way Life Should Be**

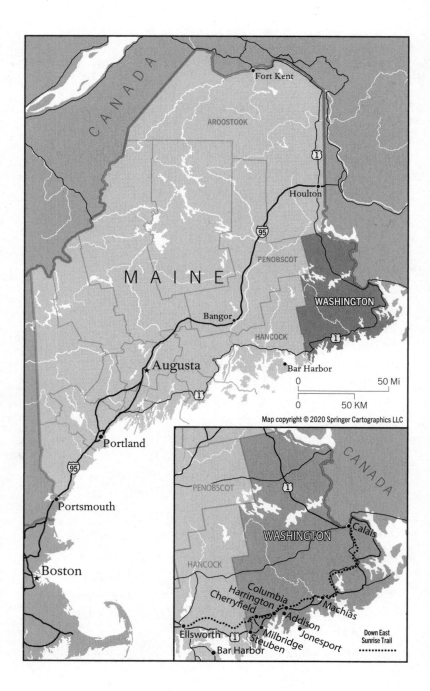

Map copyright © 2020 Springer Cartographics LLC

The Geography

The phrase "Downeast" has nautical roots that trace back to the 1800s. In summer months, ships carrying goods from Boston up the Maine coast typically sailed with a southwest wind at their backs—pushing them downwind to go eastward to their destinations. As such, sailors came to refer to the northeastern stretches of Maine as being Down East in relation to Boston. Conversely, they routinely spoke of going "up to Boston" from Down East ports, even though Boston is many miles south of Maine.

Over time, "Downeast" became a catchall phrase for the geography, culture, and distinct accent of the northern reaches of Maine's coast. Guidebooks will tell you that there's no precise southern or midpoint in the state where Downeast Maine begins; indeed, locals often use the term colloquially to describe any point east of where they are. But by the time you get far enough north to the coastal county marked in gray on the map—Washington County—you're universally acknowledged to have arrived Downeast.

Running along the Downeast corridor is a ninety-six-mile

stretch of largely pristine land known as the Sunrise Trail. Conceived as a recreational draw for nature-loving tourists, its bounty begins just below the Canadian border, in the town of Calais. From there, it tracks the jagged coast southward to the commercial enclave of Ellsworth, just north of Bar Harbor. But the portion that skirts the homes of the five girls profiled in this book is often lonely and unkempt. Here, the trail's intrinsic beauty is obscured by rocks and underbrush—and without examination, the path can be difficult to follow.

Downeast

Prologue

It's 5:00 a.m., and I'm driving up the Maine coast toward the Harrington River. I'm on the periphery of the state, and the edge of the entire nation—but in the heart of Downeast Washington County. A soft October sun has just begun to arch across the sky. The land is unforgiving: sheathed in granite, dotted by austere homes, and punctuated by low-lying brush. Around me, lobster fishermen are settling in for another day of work. Some have traveled to open waters through moonlight, eager to get a jump on their hauls. Others, in smaller boats, are just setting out. They'll hover closer to shore, or hug an inlet tucked in the jaws of the jagged coast. They'll fish like generations have before them. The waxing light will guide them to their buoys, and the sea will bring them what they need.

There are moments in life that start out feeling ordinary, until somewhere along the way, they turn out to be more extraordinary than you could ever have imagined. There are places that echo long after you've left them. And there are people, strangers at first, who end up bringing you the faith and perspective you never quite realized you were missing. So it was for me Downeast.

It's not just the region's sweeping geography—the way it feels so close to nature that you can hear its heartbeat through the trees and see its soul through the fog that dances on its skeletal coast. It's not just the feeling of being utterly alone as you wind across the Blacks Woods Road, complete with its whispered legacy of a haunting ghost named Catherine. It's the reverence with which generations of families have wrapped themselves around this place, thrived in terrain that leaves no room for idleness or self-pity, and woven a code of honor around the community they've built. They're not just from Downeast, but of it. And, despite the multiple challenges they face, there's nowhere else they'd rather be.

An hour into my early morning coastal drive, I turn off U.S. Highway 1. I make my way through the narrowing, unpaved stretch that will lead me to Harrington's Town Landing dock. When I get there, Olivia Marshall, one of the few female lobster boat captains in Downeast Maine, is standing beside her 36-foot boat, the *Gold Digger*. Olivia is in her early forties, and striking, with long blond hair, silver-blue eyes, and perfect teeth. She's been fishing since she could walk. She married a lobsterman straight out of high school, and together they raised two boys who fish. She's captained her own boat for more than fifteen years, most days with her sister Emily by her side.

We head out on the water to the first of Olivia's eight hundred traps. Both the bay and the boat are quiet, despite the presence of a dozen other working vessels. Fishermen here don't care for idle talk. Olivia will haul about a third of her traps today before she heads to shore midafternoon. Instinctively, she flicks her left-hand fingers around the *Gold Digger*'s steering wheel. Her eyes are trained on her traps, and the light creeps higher to reveal a perfect sky. She is at home.

Prologue

This is a place of seafarers and sacrifices. Where people are as tied to the whims of the water around them as human beings can be. Their sea, the Downeast sea, is a blue-hued canvas, spotted with brightly painted buoys to which the captains stake their claims. The buoy colors and patterns are unique to every owner. Admire them from afar, but don't dare to touch them if you value your limbs—as these buoys represent the fishermen's livelihood, honor, and, for many, their birthright and passage to a cherished way of life.

Here, seasons define that life. Each summer, the lobstermen glide across a steady sea, and their workdays stretch through endless sunlit hours. By the time October rolls around, they give the chilling air a knowing nod, and quicken their pace. As fall succumbs to winter's yawn, they brace their boats against the coming freeze. Months later, when they feel the ice-blown craters in the roads beneath their pickup trucks, the lobstermen know that, finally, spring has come. They hum a psalm to it, even as it swallows their muck boots in mud and pierces their ears with angry winds.

They take the hand they're dealt without fanfare or wonder. It simply is, just as it has always been.

To me, a girl from Brooklyn, the wonder is everywhere. And what I learn here is both unexpected and familiar. In every obvious way, Olivia and Emily's Downeast is as distant as could be from my Brooklyn. Their towns post population sizes that would barely fill a high-rise. Their modest homes sit on sprawling acres of largely untouched land. On a typical weekday afternoon, the corner store, post office, and library are the only open buildings on Main Street. I pass them in the blink of an eye.

But in ways that matter, I feel deeply connected to Olivia and Emily, and to this place—a place I've come to love these past

3

four years. Even though, at a superficial level, we don't appear to have much in common, I realize my foundational story is not so different from theirs.

Although my childhood memories were carved in concrete five hundred miles away, the priorities my parents emphasized mirrored many of those that shape Downeast life. At fourteen, my mom, a wide-eyed, old-world girl from a tiny Peloponnesian village, had boarded a ship from Piraeus, Greece, with her sister and crossed the Atlantic to find a new home. She and her four siblings followed their widowed father's quest for a better life. A few years later, she fell in love with my dad, a first-generation Greek American who made it through the Depression with generous daily doses of stickball and family love. My parents' story was the classic working-class immigrant tale—of hard work, sacrifice, veneration of education, heartfelt patriotism, and a relentless pursuit of the American Dream. It's a story so common to immigrant families of their time that, in its retelling, it feels almost ordinary. Even though, in the living of it, it was anything but that.

I was raised to value three things: family, education, and church. With each came aspirations and a sense of belonging. We spent our time surrounded by dozens of cousins, aunts, and uncles. We played tag in postage-stamp-size backyards. We watched football together after Sunday school. We gathered routinely in cramped, noisy dining rooms that overflowed with traditional Greek food. My parents, exceeding expectations, earned professional degrees. They each served their community through the church: Dad on the parish board, Mom as a Girl Scout leader. When my sister, brother, and I came along, they made sacrifices, not to indulge us—but to provide and be present. Together, they gave us the tools to journey as far as our dreams could take us. And we did.

Fifteen years ago, life carried me to Southwest Harbor, Maine. I'd recently met my future husband, Jeff; he had loved the Maine coast so much that the year before, he'd invested a majority of his savings to buy a home there, enabling him to divide his time, whenever he wasn't traveling for his consulting work, between a New York City studio rental and this beautiful spot. As I got to know and love him, it did not take long for me to love Maine too—and later, to want to share its coastal magnificence, and the sweep of Acadia National Park that surrounds it, with our young daughter.

Yet, the more time we spent in what became our home, and came to know the broader region, the more I became aware of a strong dichotomy between our town and those just up the coast. Because of its close proximity to Acadia, Southwest Harbor, though technically part of Downeast Maine, is vastly different from the relatively nearby places that produced the young women I would eventually meet and profile in this book.

Each year, Acadia National Park draws more than three million visitors, who collectively support nearly six thousand local jobs, and spend hundreds of millions of dollars there. Almost none of that money, or those jobs, find their way to Downeast Washington County. Indeed, Washington County—which is just as naturally beautiful, and sits barely an hour's drive from the heart of Acadia—remains one of the poorest and most isolated regions on the American Eastern Seaboard. It claims one of the highest reported rates of opioid overdoses in the nation. Many in the county struggle economically, despite a thriving lobster-fishing trade. The signs of lost industries—defunct fish-processing factories, shut-down mills, and bereft blueberry farms—are everywhere.

How could so much poverty and isolation persist so near to the bounty of Acadia—a tourist attraction that routinely attracts both busloads and billionaires? What, if anything, did the people of Downeast Washington County think of this phenomenon? And what, in the wake of so many ongoing challenges, did the future hold for their hometowns?

I started asking people around me—people like our neighbor Woody, whose family has been Downeast for generations, and whose pragmatic attitude and cheerful embrace of life's curve-balls made him, in our eyes, not just a great friend but a quint-essential Mainer. I joined Jeff as he volunteered his time to the Maine Seacoast Mission, a nonprofit that's been serving Maine's most isolated Downeast communities since 1905. Together, we came to know the mission's then president, the Reverend Scott Planting. Scott had led a set of ministries for thirty-five years in rural central Maine before turning his focus Downeast. He opened my eyes to the region's strengths and challenges, and opened doors to local leaders and educators.

I wanted to learn more. Over time, I took long drives up and down the Washington County coast. And I tried to imagine what it would be like to raise my daughter there. I sought out further connections to the area, and met dozens of Downeasters who had little reason to welcome a stranger into their midst, yet did so with kindness and open hearts.

A few months later, in November 2016, came Donald Trump's improbable electoral victory. With it came a sharp national spotlight on rural America, whose voters had played a big role in carrying him to the presidency. I'd been spending more and more time Downeast—morphing from a city girl to something of a country mom. And what I heard and read from national pundits was, for the most part, not what I saw.

Much of the postelection conversation about modern-day rural America, I came to feel, was dominated by one-dimensional preconceptions: oversimplified silhouettes of an ostensibly undereducated populace. To be sure, there were some deeper, more thoughtful efforts to recognize small-town Americans as rational actors responding to a storm of confounding challenges. These works delved into the unique contributions of and increasingly complex challenges facing citizens from remote communities, their struggle to be recognized in our nation's broader cultural, political, and policy-based discussions, and the crisis of culture that has cast a shadow on once-thriving beacons of self-preservation and communal spirit. Particularly poignant was their spotlight on the tragedies of people who are dying younger, and other long-term effects of lost industries and persistent poverty.

Many of those elements resonated with what I saw in my travels up the coast. But other aspects of the rural experience I felt went largely unrecorded—most significantly, the role of contemporary rural girls and women as central subjects for serious study—not as ancillary players, pawns, or victims, but as individuals who contribute to the American narrative in powerful, dynamic, and often positive ways. A handful of recent female-authored, rural-focused memoirs and novels have emerged in recent years, and have provided valuable, and often heart-wrenching, insights in this realm. But they have tended to be rooted in decades-old experiences, with limited focus on the challenges and opportunities of today's generation of girls growing up in rural America.

The more time I spent in Downeast Washington County,

the more I realized that the greatest clues for what's to come there—and in small towns across America—may, in fact, lie in the hearts and minds of its girls. In a region that evokes images of boys brandishing pickup trucks and old salts hauling traps, it is Downeast's girls who are most visibly wrestling with the growing complexities around them, and forging new paths both within and outside their hometowns. Their stories parallel that of millions of rural girls who face a widening generational divide and a changing economic, social, and cultural landscape as they come of age and start to make hard life choices. Their choices will determine not only their own immediate futures but also those of their struggling communities.

In the case of Downeast, girls are, by and large, surpassing the boys in academics, sports, arts, focus on community, and general ambition and leadership—and are doing so despite big challenges. Even in lobster fishing, where boys still dominate, girls are making inroads. What forces are pushing them to thrive and succeed? How has growing up in the region shaped them? And how are they helping to shape the future of their home-towns?

Serendipitously—having met many young women who are coming of age Downeast—I found myself in a position to grap-ple with these and other questions. Drawn to the community both personally and professionally, and inspired by many of the stories I was hearing, I wanted to make a contribution to the broader narrative of contemporary girls in rural America. In that spirit, I set out to help recount and memorialize what's hap-pening in one slice of the country today.

Over the next several months, I spent more and more time with young women who'd been born and raised Downeast. I chose five who collectively seemed to represent a microcosm of the goings-on of local life. These five, and dozens of others in their circles, gave me the gift of their trusting friendship and open communication, and welcomed me to join them—working on their lobster boats, praying in their churches, cheering at their sporting events, exploring their favorite campus haunts, harvesting blueberries, and reminiscing in their homes with their mothers and grandmothers. For the next four years, from their teens into their twenties, I chronicled their lives and journeys—visiting them regularly, and speaking repeatedly with family members, friends, teachers, coaches, mentors, and local leaders. Beyond these interactions, I learned about the region's economy, history, and culture through hundreds of supporting interviews, documents, and databases.

Downeast unlocks the life stories of these five girls, who, as they come of age, are caught between tradition and transformation in Washington County—and follows their journeys in this time of uncertainty. All five know the pain and joy of growing up in a region whose natural beauty and cultural stoicism mask mounting tensions around place, family, faith, and future.

Together, these girls' stories capture and exemplify the conflicts, dilemmas, and opportunities young women are facing in Downeast Maine. Willow lives in the shadow of an abusive, drug-addicted father, and searches for an elusive stability in the love she's found and the photos she takes. Vivian is a gifted writer from an established family who questions the values of her church and town, and struggles to break free without permanently severing family ties. Mckenna is a softball pitching phenom whose deepest passion is the lobster-fishing trade she learned at her father's knee. Audrey is a beloved, big-hearted high school basketball star who earns a coveted college scholarship. Josie is a confident, Yale-bound high school vale-dictorian, determined to take the world by storm.

Today's Downeast population is confronting increasing challenges—and the general perception is that much of what is good and strong seems at risk of being lost. Members of the older generations speak in hushed tones of the forces that are closing in on their beloved towns. They see dwindling populations, vanishing job opportunities, fraying families, and ravaging opioid use threatening to shatter Downeast's time-honored ways. It's a storm fomented over decades. And to those who treasure the life they've built, it often feels unstoppable.

But the paths taken by these five girls, and so many like them, give reason for hope. The journeys of Willow, Vivian, Mckenna, Audrey, and Josie shine a light on many crucial questions young women across rural America face today, and offer clues to what the future may hold—not just for them and their hometowns, but for the sixty million women, men, and children who call rural America home.

In the summer of 2019, I traveled with my husband and daughter to Greece. There, we joined my parents and uncle for a visit to Petrina, the Peloponnesian village of my mother's youth. Petrina sits on a wide plateau. Distant mountains frame its view from every angle. The Mediterranean Sea beckons some nine miles down the road, and the famed city of Sparta bustles twenty miles north.

Petrina has been around since medieval days. At times it has prospered. At times it has struggled. It has endured empires, fires, wars, and occupations. Its people are proud, industrious, and fiercely independent. It nurtures a valuable commodity in the olive oil that's drawn from a multitude of surrounding trees—a coveted asset owned by the most fortunate local multigenerational families.

These days, only a few dozen people live in the village full time, but distant links to it endure. Each summer, a thousand or so Greek Americans with generations of Petrina roots return—some for three months, others for three hours. These families swap stories about their connections to the village and share in the bounty of the olive trees that sculpt its landscape. Those who gather remember everyone and everything through the lens of Petrina's past. I, for example, am the baker's granddaughter—colloquially named "tou fournairi" ("of the baker")—and that is how my siblings, cousins, and I will always be known.

It is late afternoon in Petrina, and the summer residents are tucked away for their daily siesta. I walk across the tranquil village square, and I realize that despite the geographical and historical chasm between the Peloponnese and Downeast, the towns in these regions are not so different after all. I close my eyes and try to picture what towns Downeast will be like hundreds of years from now. I think about Willow, Vivian, McKenna, Audrey, and Josie. What mark will be left by these five smart and willful girls? How will their choices shape the lives of future generations? And what will remain of the proud, resilient communities, Downeast and beyond, that struggle today to maintain the best within them?

The challenges faced by the rural swath of our nation run deep. But hope is not lost in small-town America. Far from it. True, places like Downeast Washington County are geographically isolated, continue to struggle with persistent poverty, and lose too many in their midst to opioid addiction. But they also embody some of the strongest tenets of our American model—

through their work ethic, closeness of community, deep social capital, devotion to the natural surroundings that help sustain them, love of country, and intense drive to improve their lot in life. Not every girl will be a hero in the narrative of small-town America's survival. But the choices that rural girls make, and the paths they travel, lie at the core of what's to come. It's time, at last, to allow these girls to speak for themselves.

Part One

Daybreak

Chapter 1

The Downeast Life

Seven thousand pairs of eyes burned through Audrey Barton's heart, and she breathed deep at the free throw line. With four seconds left in the half, Audrey, the Narraguagus Lady Knights' co-captain and center, had once again reminded fans why she was the one to watch. Everything about her was lean and strong: her angular jawline; her deep brown waist-length hair, loosely swept into a ponytail; and her extended body. She picked off the ball at half court, stole a quick glance at the clock, and counted the seconds in her head. Four, three, two, one: she took the shot at the buzzer and drew the foul.

It was the 2016 Class C North state championship game, the Lady Knights' chance to bring the Gold Ball home for the first time in school history. Narraguagus was down by one point. Everyone knew the Boothbay Seahawks were favored. They were bigger—much bigger. They'd battled tougher regular-season opponents, and had emerged with a 20-1 record. But the Lady Knights were scrappy. And they had the power of Downeast pride behind them.

True, Narraguagus wasn't playing in the most competitive league in Maine's high school tournament. Big-time colleges weren't calling them. Division I scouts weren't circling their names. Those honors were reserved for Class AA teams from cities like Portland and Bangor, bright-lights places rich with talent and opportunity. The Class C teams were the small-town upstarts, whose schools struggled to keep enrollments up, whose families stretched to make ends meet. But tonight, to the nearly four thousand Downeasters who packed the Augusta Civic Center's rafters, the Lady Knights stood taller than the Boston Celtics. Barely a soul had been left at home, barely a face in their crowd was free of maroon and gold war paint, and barely a sound was heard as Audrey Barton stepped up to the foul line to try to pull the Lady Knights ahead before halftime.

When Audrey missed both free throws, she hung her head low at the bench, and whispered "I'm sorry" in a voice so pained it cracked. Olivia Marshall, the pride of Harrington, the lobster fisherman-cum-basketball coach who had shown these girls they could compete, opened her eyes wide and shook her head. "No, no, no. We're not doing that," she said as she gave Barton's arm a quick, tight squeeze. "We're good. Let's get it back together and go out there and do what we have to do. That's done and over with."

And it was.

Things stayed tight through the final minutes. Defense ruled on both sides, and baskets were scarce. Finally, forty seconds remained. Narraguagus had stretched its lead to 4 points, and the Lady Knights were jumping up and down, and almost celebrating. But Olivia Marshall knew it wasn't over. She stopped pacing long enough to gesture wildly to her head and yell, "You have to think. You have to think. You play until the final buzzer goes."

With seven seconds left in the game, the Lady Knights still led by two possessions. The Gold Ball was in their grasp, and the girls were dancing a bit as Olivia called their last time-out. "No fouls," she exhorted, fighting to check her own exhilaration. "Just let them shoot." But they were smiling, and Olivia was smiling, and she said, "Man, I'm proud of ya," and sent them on their way.

When the game ended, the roars were deafening. And the nightlong celebration began.

Every one of Harrington's 950 residents felt as if they had carried home the coveted Gold Ball. Along with neighbors from the adjoining towns of Addison, Cherryfield, Columbia, and Milbridge, they had made the five-hour round-trip drive to Augusta's Civic Center. They had followed their hometown girls since the season's late-November start, from the gym at Narraguagus, where most of them had gone to school years earlier, to Searsport, Baileyville, Jonesport, and other hamlets along the Downeast corridor. As the season chugged along and the girls ground their way toward an 18-2 season, the people here found themselves forgetting, for a couple of hours each week, about where they'd find the money for the unpaid heating bill, or how many times they'd fixed the leaking roof on their aging double-wide; about the way the money wasn't coming in so fast once blueberry raking season had come and gone; or why this year's lobster yield wasn't even close to what they needed, ever since Donny had succumbed to the lure of fentanyl; about where they'd go, without their neighbors knowing, to stock up on food for the long winter that lay ahead.

They found themselves forgetting, and they cheered for the squad with an average height of five feet five. They cheered for the multitalented coach, Olivia Marshall, who gave the girls something to strive for on and off the court. And they cheered for the possibility that this once-robust set of communities could beat the odds in other ways. Because if a group of underdog girls could lift themselves up from the valley of the overlooked, surely, they could too.

Welcome to Downeast Washington County, where the state juts so far into the Atlantic that first light routinely breaks by 5:00 a.m. Here, in the most rural county in the most rural state in the nation, is a proud, traditional place, where generations have fished lobster, raked blueberries, withstood harsh winters, and thrived amid the rugged natural beauty of their birthplace. For more than two hundred years, they have also embraced a creed of self-sufficiency, bolstered by the bonds within their communities. But now, they are struggling to navigate the changes that have overtaken their once-protected world.

By a host of metrics, there is no more challenged place in Maine than Washington County. Nearly 30 percent of its kids live in poverty, and more of those kids are persistently poor than anywhere among the New England states. Of Maine's sixteen counties, it is ranked as the least healthy, as measured by a set of factors that include behaviors, access to and quality of clinical care, education, income inequality, unemployment, family structure, and death by injury. Mortality rates from drug and alcohol abuse are significantly higher than in the rest of the state, with the fewest and farthest options for recovery. Indeed, overall life expectancy in Washington County is the lowest of Maine's counties. What's left of the population is aging, with fewer and fewer kids remaining to take their place.

To be sure, there have been boomlets, and with them prosperity for some. Downeast Maine has long been known for commercial fishing, forestry, and blueberry harvests, each bringing a century's worth of steady processing and manufacturing jobs. The lobster industry alone, a more than one-billion-dollar statewide endeavor, has sustained generations of families. It's backbreaking work, but it pays.

In recent years, though, other core employment has disappeared at alarming rates.

It's a now familiar story. Between 1970 and the early 2000s, Maine lost more than sixty thousand industrial jobs. Shifting demand and technological advances were the main offenders, forcing mills and plants into a steady retreat. What's more, a legacy of overfishing depleted the waters of virtually all breeds save the lobster—eliminating key coastal work that had long been taken for granted.

Many of those changes landed hard Downeast. Some companies that stayed retooled with new technologies, requiring fewer and more highly skilled workers. A service economy crept in, looking to fill the growing void. Instead, for most, it brought low pay and unfamiliar job demands. Economists call it a skills mismatch. Whatever you name it, the trend has helped place Washington County at the bottom of Maine state rankings of metrics for educational attainment, employment, and income. And for the residents of these towns, whose children attend Narraguagus High in dwindling numbers, social and economic forces continue to push hard against hope.

The raucous midnight celebration of the Lady Knights' championship run was on, as hundreds of proud townspeople gathered in the parking lot of Narraguagus High. At the center of the party stood Audrey Barton, star athlete, top student, hometown beauty, and a quiet, confident leader who would soon embark on the next step of her life journey at Bates College. In that moment, she epitomized optimism for the future of Downeast Maine.

A few steps away danced Willow Newenham—head held high, forgetting, for a while, the dark family secrets that she kept locked inside. A sophomore, Willow was one of two team managers for the Lady Knights. When she was with the squad, she was buoyant. With wide brown eyes, an unselfconscious overbite, and a heart-shaped face that lost definition whenever she struggled with her weight, Willow was the nurturer, the confidante, the one her teammates called "Mom." She gave the girls of Narraguagus basketball her heart, and they gave her the family she never had.

Not far from Willow, Mckenna Holt flashed her brilliant smile and basked in the knowledge that she was one of only two freshman players to earn court time for the championship game. A gifted athlete, she could already begin to imagine the moment when she might lead the Lady Knights to statewide glory again.

Off in one of the celebration's outer rings stood Vivian Westford, absorbing the scene with a wry and distant smile, contemplating just the right moment to slip away for another adventure beyond the community's watchful eyes. Beneath the surface of Vivian's childlike visage lay a well of emotional journeys. Too many for a sixteen-year-old to have withstood unscarred.

Finally, Josie Dekker. Proud, wholesome, virtuous Josie. She locked arms with those around her in tribute to the team. Yet simultaneously, in manner and deed, she stood apart and seemingly above the crowd.

They were, that night, five girls who individually personified and collectively represented a microcosm of the Downeast life. Audrey, Vivian, and Mckenna claimed multigenerational legacies in the region, and surnames that opened doors and held a trove of local lore. They were shaped in powerful ways by these legacies, both embracing and rebelling against them. Josie, on the other hand, was a relative newcomer, whose grandparents had abandoned their Pennsylvania roots in search of a "simpler country life"—who, decades later, were still defining their space in the taxonomy of Downeast culture. Willow was a local girl of a different sort, whose family name brought sidelong glances. When the celebration ended, Willow would face an amalgam of challenges not uncommon in the region. And yet she cherished this place despite the pain she endured within it.

Different as they were, and distinct as the choices were that each would make in the coming years, these five girls were alike in fundamental ways. They shared a common bond of Downeast identity that made them, above all else, resilient. They saw their birthplace for all its flaws, and yet remained reverent of the place they called home, and of the gifts of nature and community it bestowed on them. They not only accepted but embraced the work ethic that came with the life. And although they occasionally grumbled about the geographic isolation, the lack of movie theaters, and the paltry restaurant options, they were Downeasters through and through. Even if they planned to leave—for school, love, adventure, or warmer climates—they'd stay forever tied to this region. What was it about this place, and its people, that captured their very souls?

At 2:00 a.m., the crowd, still toasting hope in the high school parking lot, began to disperse. There was work to be done. There were needs to be met, and elements to battle, on land and at sea. Morning's first light would soon emerge, and with it a stinging reminder of the troubles that sat like a weight atop this proud and tight-knit community.

Chapter 2

Beginnings

By twelve years old, Willow Newenham was lost in the wreckage of a crumbling childhood. A few days after her father's hospital discharge, she hid in her room, hoping for a night of peace. But the damage was done, the finger had been crushed, and there was no turning back from the rage that had begun to descend on the brown house on Valley Lane. Willow had sensed it building since even before the accident. And when William Newenham's torrent came, the only thing standing between Willow's two younger brothers and a merciless pounding was Mom.

It wasn't the first time, nor would it be the last. But the ferocity of the beatings after Dad's accident, the bloody result of a truck jack gone awry at Powell's Lobster plant, was evidence to Willow that the Newenham family had entered uncharted waters.

In Willow's world, the same story played over and over again. Dad got high, Dad beat Mom, Dad went after the boys. Most of the time he didn't get to Willow. But sometimes she wondered if the mental abuse he routinely subjected her to was worse.

They called it their "family secret."

It echoed through the walls of their cramped rooms. Sister and brothers surrendered to it, and it bound them together. No one else in this tight community could know because, in the family's eyes, "we would be banned."

And it was "just fine," remembered Willow. "I didn't say anything, and that's how life went on."

But it wasn't fine.

When Willow was born, William and Lily were students at Narraguagus High. Lily was eighteen, William was sixteen, and with the news of Lily's pregnancy, Lily's mother insisted there was no choice in the matter. The pair married at the local church and began to raise their baby girl. They called her their "wonderful terrible mistake."

When Willow was one, Lily worked the night shift as an aide at a local nursing home. William worked mornings, mostly day labor on the waterfront, and he and Lily took turns watching the baby. Years later, Lily told Willow that she arrived home one night to find William high on cocaine, shaking Willow hard and fast. Lily had to beat him to make him let go.

After Willow's first brother, Scott, was born, Lily begged William to get a vasectomy. He promised he would, but not long after, Lily was pregnant again. One night, in Lily's first trimester, William got high again. "He knew she was pregnant with my Isaac, my younger brother, and he beat her to the point where she thought she was gonna lose the baby. She and him were the only ones that knew."

Most locals thought it was the drugs that made him do it, but Willow knew it wasn't. Sober or not, it was his way. It was pretty much the one thing Willow could count on in her early life. "I saw my dad beat my mom so many times," she remembered. "I have this one visual I can never get out of my head. My dad ripping my mom's hair as he drags her across the floor. And he wasn't even high. My entire life I wish that I could blame it on him being high. But I can't."

There was a time, when Isaac was still a baby, that things felt vaguely settled in the Newenham home. Lily and William were working carpentry together, taking whatever jobs would come their way. They'd moved from the trailer park to a house in Harrington. It wasn't much to look at, but at least it was a house, a place to begin to put down roots. Not long after, the Newenhams cheered their good fortune when they found they could afford a better place, one town over, in Cherryfield. It was, recalled Willow, "the nicest house we'd lived in, and we all got along for a while, and everything was good."

This too would end. It wasn't long before Willow learned that "Dad had been cheating on Mom." He'd left the house on Christmas Day to spend time with the woman he'd been seeing on the side. "And Mom broke down." It turned out, too, that William's drug use and drinking hadn't let up. "He was a mean drunk," Willow remembered, and when he'd arrive home out of control, Willow learned to scramble to her parents' bedroom. As Willow hid, Lily would do her best to protect her little girl. Indeed, for a time, that bedroom became Willow's safe haven, so much so that Willow took to sleeping there regularly with her mom, while William slept in Willow's room.

When Willow was seven, William brought home a dirt bike for her birthday. Willow never knew where he got the money for it. Dirt bikes weren't cheap, and William wasn't working much. It was exactly the bike Willow had dreamed of owning—bright red, with black handlebars and knobby tires—and when William gave it to her, she felt a rare sense of joy.

The feeling didn't last. Lily would later tell Willow about the day it was lost. How they had peered out to the driveway and seen two strangers approaching. How, on its face, the presence of strangers at the Newenham home might not have been alarming to anyone—after all, throughout Willow's childhood, characters seemed to come and go regularly. But how this time was different.

It needn't have been a surprise to the Newenhams when the strangers yelled that they were there for their money: two thousand dollars, to be exact. William had promised them, one too many times, that he was good for it, in exchange for the drugs they'd fronted him. But this time, it seemed, he'd pushed his luck too far, in the way that would later become all too familiar to Willow. And now he had hell to pay. Lily watched as arms flailed and voices rose. She held her daughter close as Willow watched the two men grab her dirt bike and haul it away. She cried so hard and long that, eventually, Lily told her, *You need to stop. Because those people were here to kill us if your dad didn't pay.* So it was that Willow came to learn that nothing good was ever meant to last.

After William crushed his finger on the job, his doctor prescribed hydrocodone to ease his pain. It quickly became William's drug of choice. He started taking more and more pills, to the point where, as Willow recalled, there was a near-constant otherworldly look in his eyes. "My mom used to say that hydros were Dad's candy. We'd watch, and he'd just keep eating them." His physical abuse of Lily and the boys continued. His mental torment of Willow intensified. His habit threatened to destroy them all.

He wasn't alone. From 2016 to 2018, Washington County had, by far, the highest rate of drug overdoses of any county in Maine. From 2012 to 2017, the number of drug-affected babies born in the county increased by nearly 50 percent. And even though these statistics are the most reliable countywide numbers around, experts agree they underestimate the scope of the problem. Statewide, from 2013 to 2017, the rate of drug-based fatalities more than doubled, moving Maine's national overdose death rate ranking from thirty-second to eighth highest of the fifty states. Ask local residents to describe their feelings about living here, and they'll gush about their love of the natural beauty, their unassailable bonds to community, land, and sea. Then they'll pause and tell you about a parent, sibling, cousin, grandparent, or friend who's hooked. And the fear of what their towns are losing washes over them.

When life got particularly rough at the Newenhams', Lily would turn to her mom for help in caring for Willow, while keeping the two boys at home. As a result, Willow ended up living with her maternal grandmother, Grandma Ann, on and off for the first twelve years of her life. In between, she was shuttled back to the various spots that her mom and dad called home. She moved seven times before she was eight.

Not long after the seventh move, Willow met Vivian Westford. By reputation, the Westfords were about as far from the Newenhams as a family in Harrington could be. The Westfords were the sort of multigenerational Downeasters who routinely drew a nod of approval and a firm handshake at the corner store. As if to say, "Hats off to you. *You* are the backbone of Harrington—the kind of family that brings pride to our town." Indeed, there was plenty of history on which to rest that pride. Vivian's great-grandfather had helped establish Narraguagus High in the late 1960s, and had served as the school district's superintendent. Her grandfather, Sam, grew his first local business, Westford Oil, so successfully that it would set up his kids for a lifetime of financial stability, as long as they were smart and frugal. He and his wife, Louise, went on to create Hartvale Farms. Together, they raised five kids on the farm and cultivated more than two hundred acres of wild blueberry barrens. To supplement their wholesale business, they opened a retail store. They sold cranberries, grapes, vegetables, shiitake mushrooms, and balsam products—and offered tours to anyone who showed the slightest interest.

When Vivian's father came of age, he displayed the promise of a boy who would uphold the Westford name. He earned a scholarship to the University of Maine at Orono (UMO), and graduated with two bachelor's degrees, one in biology and another in botany. It was more than most families in these parts could claim for two generations. He would later go on to run farm operations at a major wild blueberry producer and distributor, and serve multiple times as a town selectman.

The Westfords were a proud and productive bunch. There were plenty of them around—twenty-three all told, between grandparents, aunts, uncles, and cousins—and pretty much all of them had an active hand in the farm and a prime seat on Sundays at the Lighthouse Baptist Church. Louise was the matriarch of the family, and a take-no-prisoners leader in the church. Vivian grew up as an only child among watchful eyes, with a high bar for moral standards and a strict code of conduct at home. Chores were to be done promptly, backtalk was prohibited, and piercings, tattoos, suggestive clothing, and alcohol were strictly off-limits. From the age of eight, Vivian regularly helped out at Hartvale Farms, first raking blueberries and later packing and lifting the fruit-laden 50-pound crates up onto dusty pickup trucks. After the blueberry season waned, she'd turn to sorting fish for her parents' sideline bait business.

Vivian and Willow met in first grade, at Harrington Elementary School. There, they locked on to each other in the cosmic way by which girls that age know they're meant to be best friends. For Willow, first grade was a forced redux—a second shot at the learning that her home life had stolen from her. Willow was the girl who stood with her back to the wall and clenched her fists until her knuckles ached. She had a doughy frame that was adorned by unremarkable clothes, and every day she anticipated the inevitability of the unexpected.

Vivian was unlike Willow in all the obvious ways. Her parents showered her with encouragement and attention, and she, in turn, emerged as an open and confident child. She had the kind of presence that made her teachers lean a little closer. Her mind was ethereal, and she captivated. Her soft face was punctuated by almond-shaped, emerald eyes that danced a little as she spoke, and her smile was deep and slightly asymmetric. She exuded a vulnerability that almost instantly invited a hug.

The girls began their journey hand in hand. On the school playground, Willow distanced herself from others. "She'd run away from people, because she had a lot going on," remembered Vivian. But together, they made their own space. They hid in the purple tube slide and wrote their names and "cuss words" on the worn, wooden posts that tethered it. They shared a seat on the school bus home. "It was a long ride," recalled Vivian, "and when we got there, we'd run outside and play as long as we were able."

To those who paid attention, Willow and Vivian made an improbable pairing. But it worked.

Sometimes, Vivian would meet up with other neighborhood

kids, and Willow would join the group for an outdoor adventure. Together, they'd routinely test the boundaries of their bodies against nature—foraging in the woods, riding bikes past town limits along the Sunrise Trail, and cannonballing into the river off jagged overhangs.

Vivian and Willow loved the feeling of freedom that came with those adventures—the embrace of the sloping earth around them, the touch of the grass beneath their feet. The blades slurped their ankles and swallowed their toes. The sun chased the chill from their bodies and practically lifted them across open fields. And in those moments, all that mattered was the endless possibility of a perfect day.

There were, however, plenty of days that weren't perfect. Especially for Willow. There was too much violence and uncertainty; there were too many drugs and distant looks. Those times, when she hid in her room, or packed a bag for another indefinite stay with Grandma Ann, Willow came to understand that this was her normal. She'd hunker down and remind herself that, sooner or later, the storm would pass.

It was when Willow and Vivian were apart that Vivian forged a different sort of friendship with Josie Dekker.

Josie was the second youngest of four girls, born into a tight-knit, hardworking, church-going family. As a child, Josie, much like her older two sisters, was filled with promise and poise. She grew up in Cherryfield, which has been around since the late 1600s, and today is home to some 1,100 residents. It boasts a proud but long-defunct logging history, and a string of associated families who were once considered well-to-do. Home to the largest wild blueberry manufacturers in the nation, Cherryfield calls itself the Blueberry Capital of the World.

Beginnings

Josie and Vivian met in preschool at the Lighthouse Church. Their grandmothers, Mae and Louise, who could reliably be found at services every Sunday, had been friends for years. Josie and Vivian learned at an early age to be the model citizens their family and church expected them to be: to sit quietly as the pastor darted from page to page in the King James Bible, exhorting his parishioners to follow along; to march dutifully into Sunday school and heed the rules invoked by their teacher; to supplement their Christian education at Vacation Bible School in the summer; and to respect, in sequence, their Lord, their parents, and their church elders.

At church, Vivian, Josie, and the minister's daughter, Chloe, were inseparable. The three formed a secret group—the Bumble Bee Club—whose core activities included collecting ladybugs and other insects, staging sippy-cup tea parties, and "stinging" Chloe's two older brothers, who sat in the pews in front of them. "We spent a lot of time together, the three of us," remembered Vivian. "At church, we sat in the same row as Grammy Pat." Grammy Pat, who lacked blood ties to any of the three, was a fixture at the fundamentalist Baptist church. "She was deaf, with giant glasses. The type of lady you'd imagine handing out candy and paper to kids, to keep us occupied. And she'd speak right up, right over the minister's voice, during prayer. She passed recently, but she was loved." The Bumble Bee Club lasted through the girls' grammar school years. "We had great times," recalled Vivian wistfully.

So it unfolded, that starting at an early age, Vivian formed a set of parallel experiences—gliding between romps with Willow and measured playdates with Josie. The two paths worked for a while for Vivian, so much so that her memories of childhood until age ten were marked by contentment—a sense that her Downeast life, despite the austerity of it, was somewhat magical. In time, things would change, as they always do, and life for Vivian, Willow, and Josie would grow more textured—and more complicated. Change was a natural consequence of growing up, even in a place as willfully timeless as Downeast.

Chapter 3

Girls Gone Fishing

When Phoebe Holt learned she was having a baby girl, she thought, *Oh God, no.*

God, no, she whispered to herself. *There's just nothing in this area for her. She's going to grow up, pack up, and move away.*

Phoebe didn't remember feeling the same way a dozen years earlier, when she was pregnant with Matthew, her firstborn. Or even before that, when things had begun to get serious with Jake, and he'd taken the step of introducing her to Dylan, his son from a previous relationship. Those boys had their Downeast future pretty much mapped out for them. As long as they were able-bodied—and willing to chase the sunrise each morning— they could fish. After all, Jake was a fisherman, and a good one at that. What's more, Jake and Phoebe had smarts, drive, and the good sense not to fritter their earnings away. Jake's beginnings had been humble, but he'd been determined as heck to someday earn enough to own a commercial fishing wharf. Not just any wharf, but one that would thrive under the banner of his family name. In Phoebe, he'd found a wife and partner who was equally ambitious—and just as willing to put in the work it took to get there.

When Matthew came along, Jake was still digging clams for a living, and helping run a friend's lobster boat. By the time Matthew turned two, Jake had earned and saved enough to buy his own fishing boat, which he aptly named *Dylan & Matthew*. Not long after, he traded up to a 58-footer and switched for a while from lobstering to quahogging. For the next decade or so, leading up to Mckenna's birth, Jake kept working and saving, with Phoebe by his side. Once Dylan and Matthew were ready to work full time, Jake's stake in the fishing game would give the boys a solid place to start. The rest was up to them.

But Mckenna, little Mckenna. What lay ahead for her? Phoebe, whose family roots, like Jake's, were local, could tell you exactly what. A slot as an aide at the nursing home; or maybe, if she had the wherewithal to get credentialed, a teaching job at a nearby school. They weren't bad options, Phoebe knew, but they didn't pay much. Certainly not enough to comfortably raise a family— especially if she'd wind up having to do it on her own. Even with a college education, which Jake and Phoebe were dead set on making available to Mckenna, the pickings were slim for girls who stayed Downeast.

Thinking back to her own youth, Phoebe sighed. She'd grown up raking blueberries, and had helped out with whatever jobs might bring in extra cash. When she graduated from Narraguagus High, she'd gone to work full time at her uncle Sebastian's wreath factory. For years leading up to that time, Phoebe's dad and Sebastian had been partners in a concrete business. Then Sebastian had decided to go out on his own, and tried his luck at cultivating balsam for wreathmaking. The nearby forests were rich with balsam, and land was cheap. The gamble paid off. Before long, he'd built his wreath company into a multimillion-dollar venture. Phoebe's parents, on the other hand, made do through their own endeavors, but there was no way they had enough to send Phoebe and her four brothers to college.

Along the way, Phoebe had met Jake, and the pair started dating. Phoebe was nineteen when she learned she was pregnant with Matthew. At first, she and Jake considered getting married, but they decided it might be better to hold off for a while and see how things turned out. Time proved Jake to be a good man and an attentive father. And so, when Matthew turned two, the couple had decided to wed, and set on their way to building a solid life together.

It took twelve years for Mckenna to follow her big brother, but when she did, it didn't take long for Phoebe to realize she needn't have worried about her daughter's future. Even as a toddler, that girl was quick and strong, and full of spunk. "Lo and behold," remembered Phoebe, "right away, Mckenna figured things out. She watched her dad and her brothers out on that boat. And she wasn't about to be left behind."

By the time Mckenna was five, Phoebe could see it, plain as day. Mckenna Holt was born to fish.

In the handful of years that followed, Mckenna wasted no time preparing to join the ranks of Downeast lobster fishermen. She found a fishing soul mate, and best friend, in Noah Marshall. Noah was the second son of Narraguagus alumni and high school sweethearts Brady and Olivia Marshall (later of Gold Ball basketball fame). Brady and Olivia were a formidable husband and wife lobster-fishing team, and by the time their two boys had come along, they knew they were headed toward a multi-boat family enterprise.

As it went, when the Marshall kids, Noah and his older brother, Finn, were small, Olivia had turned to Brady, whom she loved dearly but didn't abide taking orders from on a fishing boat, and said, "I'm ready to captain my own boat." It was a bold move—something only a handful of women in the state, let alone Downeast, had done before. It raised a few eyebrows, to be sure, but Olivia was determined to make a go of it.

No sooner had Olivia gotten her boat than little Finn had turned to Olivia's dad and said, "I want my own boat too." So Neil Landry built Finn a miniature lobster boat. It was eight feet long, with a switch, and a small trolling motor. They even had traps for it. Neil painted it blue, just like his own boat, *Easy Money*, and named it *River Brat*.

When Finn outgrew the *River Brat*, the Marshalls passed it on to Noah and Mckenna. The pair spent countless hours on that boat—out on the lake, and in the offseason, in the Marshalls' dooryard. They'd also climb onto Olivia's boat when she wasn't looking, and imagine how glorious it would be to fish on a life-size vessel. It was a sight worthy of remark. Playing at lobster fishing all summer long might've been somewhat typical behavior for a Downeast boy. But not for a girl.

Then again, Mckenna Holt wasn't your typical girl. She wasn't one to pass up a challenge, and she hated to lose. A stunning child, she was wrapped in a compact frame, with bright blue eyes and a ruddy, square-jawed face. She had her father's features and his tenacity. Indeed, father and daughter were so alike that locals took to calling Mckenna "Jake with a ponytail."

The seeds for Mckenna's future were planted well before she was born, and her ties to the Marshall family were generational. Fathers Jake Holt and Brady Marshall had grown up as friends and neighbors. Even before Jake and Brady were born, *their* parents had faced such tough times that they had pooled their money and shared a house to make ends meet. Both boys came from long-standing Downeast stock, into families that made their living, one way or another, from the sea.

From childhood, Jake, who was one year older than Brady, had had a penchant for fast boats and easy trouble. Whenever the weather allowed it, Jake would head down to the lake. Brady and his brother would often go with him. The boys would hop on the back of Jake's speedboat and into a "tubes double," two inner tubes tied to a line and attached to the back of the boat. Almost immediately, Jake would rev up his engine and do his best to flip them.

"C'mon up," Jake would taunt. "You're not scared, are ya?"

He'd let the two boys ride for a minute, then whip them around doing a hundred or better, and dump them off. Their bodies would hit the water with a crash so loud you'd swear they were hitting pavement.

One summer afternoon, Brady jumped on the tubes double, determined, this time, not to get thrown.

"Let 'er rip," Brady called out.

"If you say so," replied Jake, as he gunned the motor to its breaking point.

Within seconds, Brady's brand-new nylon Nike shorts were looped around his ankles. But Jake paid him no mind. He kept going, once more around the lake, just long enough to make a spectacle of Brady.

As Brady came off the tubes, he yelled, "Jake, ya did it this time. Ya made me lose my shorts."

"Hah," laughed Jake, "Twinkletoes got his rudder out trying to steer."

Years later, after Mckenna was born, the Holt lake tradition continued. Jake, despite his advancing age, was still subjecting friends and family to his "tubes-double" rite of passage. Mckenna was no exception. Jake expected her to participate, pretty much as soon as she could swim. At first, friends and family speculated that, by bringing Mckenna along for the ride, Jake would be more cautious. Instead, he barreled through the water twice as fast. Sure enough, as soon as Mckenna clambered on to a tube, she'd be catapulted.

Jake pushed the limit with nearly everything he touched. He jacked up trucks. He souped up ATVs and snowmobiles. The combination of long winters and proximity to the Sunrise Trail made snowmobiling, in particular, an ideal local pastime; even cash-strapped families often mustered the funds or incurred the debt to buy a vehicle or two to navigate the rough terrain. When Mckenna's turn came to have a snowmobile of her own, Jake nearly tripled the maximum speed on it—from 8 to 22 miles an hour—and sent her spirit, and sometimes her body, soaring.

Jake would say it was all in good fun. He also knew it would toughen Mckenna for the life that lay ahead. True to form, Mckenna didn't just take it in stride. She embraced it.

When Mckenna turned eight, as soon as the law allowed it, she got her student fishing license. But much to her chagrin, the law also required her to take a backseat to her brothers—to fish as an apprentice, with a limited number of traps, until she'd logged one thousand hours of fishing. Those early years would mark the first and last time Mckenna agreed to step aside for boys.

It was also around her eighth year that Mckenna started playing softball. Phoebe wasn't surprised to see how well, and quickly, Mckenna took to the game. As a girl, Phoebe, too, had excelled in sports. She'd co-captained every team she'd played on at Narraguagus—volleyball, basketball, and softball. At the close of her senior year, she'd won the high school's Co-Athlete of the Year award. After, Phoebe made it a point to keep sports in her life however she could. When Mckenna started elementary school and Phoebe returned to Narraguagus as a substitute teacher, she also started coaching junior high girls' basketball.

Still, even as Phoebe spread her time and talent through the community, she kept her attention trained on Mckenna. Indeed, she'd been the force behind Mckenna's early entry into softball. But despite Mckenna's promise at the game, her relationship with it got off to a rocky start, and she nearly quit soon after she first picked up a glove. Mckenna would stand in the outfield, where the coach had positioned her, and grumble to herself about being so far from the action. After a couple of seasons, she turned to Phoebe and said, "I just want to pitch, because pitchers get to touch the ball all the time. I just want to be able to play." She poured her heart into pitching, and soon she was trekking forty-five minutes to Ellsworth every Sunday morning to work with Jed Peters, a private coach who was known through eastern Maine as the "guru of softball pitching." With softball, as with all else she tackled, Mckenna Holt was determined to work harder, and be better, than everyone around her.

When Mckenna turned ten, Jake and Phoebe moved the family seven miles down the road, from Columbia Falls to Harrington. Their new home was set high on a hill, with eight acres of land and breathtaking views of Pleasant Bay. The sweep of blue that lay before them made the spot a prime location for the couple's long-imagined Holt's Wharf. No doubt about it. Jake and Phoebe had arrived.

Soon after, as the Holts were still settling into their new life, Mckenna turned to her dad and asked, "Can I set my traps yet?" It wasn't the first time she'd posed the question to Jake, but each time before, she'd held her breath for his response and had been disappointed. Now, Jake smiled and motioned toward his boat and said, "Here ya go, Mckenna." And away they went.

One town over, thirteen-year-old Audrey Barton was loading up the *No Interest*, the lobster boat she shared with her brother Mark. With only fifteen months separating Audrey and Mark, the pair was practically inseparable. But while Mark was dead set on lobstering full time after high school, Audrey dreamt of a time when she'd no longer have to haul. Indeed, Audrey and Mark's boat was named in recognition of exactly how Audrey felt about fishing. She'd done it, dutifully, for the past year, alongside her dad, two brothers, four uncles, and a half dozen cousins, give or take. But unlike most of them, she wasn't defined by it.

What did define Audrey was the way she handled everything she encountered with a calm and gentle assuredness. People who knew her were apt to say that, in all of Downeast Maine, they'd be hard pressed to find someone warmer, kinder, or humbler than Audrey Barton.

Audrey was born twenty-six months after her parents lost their five-year-old daughter, Hannah, in a searing tragedy. It was a Saturday afternoon in March, and aunts, uncles, cousins, and grandparents had just begun to assemble for one of the extended family's frequent gatherings, which always took place at one Barton home or another. On this particular Saturday, the first hints of winter thaw had emerged, and the kids had tumbled out of the house and into the driveway to play. No one thought much of it as ten-year-old Daniel Barton hopped on an ATV. Plenty of Downeast boys and girls his age drove ATVs—it was fully legal as long as they wore helmets. Steps away, Hannah unknowingly moved into her cousin's path, and at that moment, there was no pulling back for either child. Thirty-six hours later, Hannah was gone, and all that was left was a grief so powerful it barreled through the heart of every Barton along the Back Bay Road.

In the aftermath, Mike and Suzanne Barton regained their footing, and found, in Audrey, a second-chance girl. And although she'd been conceived in heartbreak, from the moment Audrey arrived, her presence was lighter than air. For as long as she could remember, Audrey recognized the symbolism of her very existence. Not as a burden, she'd be quick to say, but as a somber point of pride. As a child, she saw it in the subtleties of adults around her—the soulful glances and lingering embraces. She sensed it before she could fully grasp it, that universal language of sympathy for those who endure the unimaginable.

At home, Hannah's too-short life—and absence—were woven into the fabric of Barton family life. It was never a conversation her parents had to sit down and have with Audrey. It was, rather, a deeply felt truth, that Audrey was on earth, and Hannah was in heaven. As a child, Audrey memorized the contours of Hannah's face from the photos of her that graced nearly every room in the house. They sat unassumingly alongside those of Audrey and her brothers. She played with Hannah's toys and wore Hannah's hand-me-downs. So it was that Hannah was always with her. And it felt, to Audrey, more like a comfort than a loss.

In the years that followed, Audrey, Mark, and their older brother, Charlie, grew up in a home where love overcame sorrow. The family ate together, played together, and laughed and cried together, in between the ardor of life. They also thrived.

The roots of the Barton family ran deep in Milbridge,

a maritime town of 1,300 people that hugs the banks of the Narraguagus River. Four generations of Bartons lived on the Back Bay Road, in a dozen homes with crisscrossing land, with more structures rising as grandkids began to have kids of their own. Audrey's paternal grandfather, Michael, had been a jack of nearby trades: a sandworm and clam digger, woodsman, farmer, and eventually, a lobstering sternman for his son. Audrey's paternal grandmother, Sarah, could trace her Back Bay roots to her parents' and grandparents' days. Until the day Sarah died, she herself had spent much of her eighty-three years in the house with the barn at the top of the hill, tending to her horses and teaching her daughters and granddaughters the art and skill of barrel racing.

Audrey's parents met at an early age and dated while both attended Narraguagus High. They married not long after. At about that time, Mike and his brother, Doug, had discovered the possibility of profit in lobster fishing. The work suited them, and by the 1990s, they and their families had begun a steady march up the income ladder. Suzanne earned a culinary certificate, and returned to Narraguagus High as a cafeteria cook. Then came the loss of Hannah. Mike was doing well enough to allow Suzanne to quit her job. Her three remaining kids needed her. And she needed to know she'd be there for them.

Mike worked long hours, and even longer seasons, lobstering off the Milbridge coast. He was, in work and life, a model of caution and self-discipline. He had to be if he wanted to succeed as a self-employed fisherman. Mike and Suzanne expected Audrey and her brothers to contribute; each child fished, summers into autumns, from an early age. Mike and Suzanne also expected the kids to do their homework as soon as they got home, help out with chores, and attend church and Sunday school regularly.

With these and other rules in the Barton household, Audrey, Mark, and Charlie didn't negotiate. They simply did as they were told.

Audrey grew up comfortable by Downeast standards, above the dividing line that separates boat-owning lobster-fishing families from the rest. She swam in the pool in her backyard, traveled regularly to Ellsworth and Bangor for sports and activities, and camped with her family in Acadia for one week each summer. Following in the steps of two generations of Barton girls before her, Audrey also had her own horse—a rescue from a family friend. Dobie, as the horse was called, arrived just before Audrey's eleventh birthday, and boarded at her grandmother's barn next door. For the next six years, Audrey competed regularly in Maine-based rodeos.

But her passion quickly became basketball.

She started playing when she was eight, mostly by tagging along with her dad and brothers. Mike coached the Milbridge elementary and middle school basketball teams, with weekday practices from four to seven o'clock on an aging basketball court at the old Town Hall. Most nights, Audrey and Mark would beg Mike to linger after practice so they could keep shooting baskets. "There's no heat in here," Mike would say. "You'll freeze if we stay much longer." "Please, please," they'd respond as they pulled their gloves tighter and tucked their hats closer around their dancing eyes. "Can't we play just a little bit more?"

In middle school, Audrey joined a regional travel team. The girls named themselves the Pink Panthers, and bonded on long bus rides across lonely roads. By eighth grade, she added a regular three-hour round trip north to Old Town to her already packed schedule—to compete in the Eastern Maine Amateur Athletic Union (AAU) league. By the time Audrey began high school, barely a day passed when she wasn't holding a basketball in her hands.

At Narraguagus, Audrey was an obvious pick for the varsity team. She was a veteran player before she even set foot on the high school court, and she towered over most of the girls in the school. She was also a natural leader—patient and soft spoken, but capable of tamping down the inevitable drama that crept into practices and games. With these qualities, it didn't take long for Audrey to emerge as the Lady Knights' star center. Then came Olivia Marshall—back onto the Narraguagus basketball court, only this time as the girls' coach. Marshall quickly earned the respect of her girls, just as she had with the fishermen whose trade she shared. Two years into her stint as varsity coach, with that respect in hand, she coached her team across the Gold Ball finish line.

It was around the time of the Lady Knights' championship win that Audrey learned she had been admitted to Bates College. Bates hadn't been the only school eyeing Audrey. Her profile, on and off the court, had made her a strong regional prospect. As interest from schools intensified, Audrey had begun to key in on her Maine-based options; she wasn't particularly interested in venturing beyond the state line. On paper, Bates was a dream match. It would give Audrey a top-notch liberal arts education and a chance to play college ball. And it didn't hurt that Bates had thrown in a needs-based scholarship. The extra funds wouldn't cover everything, but they'd at least put a dent in the school's hefty tuition. In truth, Audrey thought, there was little more she could have asked for or expected. Her hard work had paid off, her family and community were beaming with pride, and her next adventure was about to begin.

Chapter 4

Pillars

Vivian's second childhood, as she later called it, began when she was ten. It came with the news of her parents' split—the stunning realization that Max and Emma, as such, would cease to exist. Vivian would long remember the day their unit of three was shattered, as her parents "fell somewhere between relief and misunderstanding" and she, "the littlest one, fell but did not land."

Max remarried soon after the divorce. Vivian felt bludgeoned, as Caroline, her father's new wife, entered her world. At Dad's house, Max and Caroline were blissful, but all Vivian felt was misery. At Mom's house, the first of a series of homes that she would rent for Vivian and herself, Emma wrapped herself in depression. To help pay the bills, she added more hours at work. With Vivian, she'd tried to assume the mantle of heroic single mom. But more often than not, Emma wound up immobile on her couch at the end of a long workday, while Vivian amused herself with coloring books on the floor nearby. As hours passed, Vivian watched her mother for signs of hope. "I can still smell it," Vivian would later reflect, "maternal depression, hanging from my little body, and I now know why I began to feel so tired too."

In time, Vivian would learn the history of her mother's family, the layers of it that coursed through her veins and mingled with her elite Westford blood. Vivian's maternal grandmother, Claire, had grown up in a house riddled with domestic violence, often watching helplessly as her father beat her mother. Claire had also taken on the responsibility of raising her five younger siblings. Years later, Claire's father—Vivian's great-grandfather—had attempted suicide. He was ultimately institutionalized in a Bangor psychiatric hospital. When Claire's time came to marry, she fell into an all too common cycle of despair—with an abusive husband whose reach extended to his two daughters. Vivian's Aunt Lynette, who was stricken with cerebral palsy, bore the brunt of her father's damage. Emma, the younger of the two, built a fortress in a corner of her mind, one that still holds unlocked secrets of those early days.

Sometime before Emma's thirteenth birthday, Claire had arrived home from work to find that her husband had packed up his things and left. The only saving grace was that he never returned. With barely enough to support her girls, Claire went back to school to become a teacher, and raised Emma and Lynette in a small one-story house in Cherryfield. This was the house that Vivian would retreat to as a child whenever she craved pancakes and grandmotherly warmth. "You could throw a rock from one side of Mam's house to the other, and it wasn't much to look at from the outside, but I loved going there," Vivian recalled.

At the time of Emma and Max's divorce, a generation after Claire's, the young Vivian barely knew the secrets of her mother's family. She only knew, when she saw Emma in distress, that she, a little girl, was powerless to ease her own pain, let alone her mother's. So in those rough early years after her parents' divorce, the turmoil that followed Vivian seared her heart.

But she was a Westford, and to outside eyes, she remained the proud and persevering girl, the rising beacon, she'd always been. The Westford legacy had dictated Vivian's place in the Downeast world, and her childhood comportment had sealed it. Vivian knew it was a legacy that would take her far, within the confines of Downeast Washington County. But dig a little deeper, and things got complicated. True, Vivian reflected, she could use the Westford name to get pretty much anything she wanted. She never did take advantage of her station in local life—beyond the superficial perk or two—but she took some comfort in knowing that she could. That said, as Vivian grew, she began to realize that the gifts of her station came with a price. Expectations were carved in stone. To crumble was to let a whole town down. And yet, Vivian could feel herself disintegrating from the inside out. Perhaps, she began to think, her pillars weren't as foundational as they seemed. Perhaps it was only a matter of time before they'd fall in a heap to the ground.

Time marched on. Emma and Max stopped speaking to each other, and the severed relationship continued to take its toll on Vivian. It wasn't until Vivian's teenage years that she sensed the unraveling spool inside that had been set into motion by her parents' divorce. Not long after her thirteenth birthday, Vivian's feelings started to cascade. To ease the hurt, she began to write. Long entries in a journal at home. Personal confessions meant for no one's judgment but her own. She also began to cut herself. Today, the scars on her legs remain, fading reminders of adolescent angst. But Vivian, ever a Westford, hid them well.

In her early teenage years, the one friend Vivian confided in was Willow. The pair would routinely bound off the school bus, run to Vivian's house—where Willow would spend time when she wasn't shuttling between her grandparents' homes—and share their secrets. Those were protected moments, when the girls found comfort in sharing fragments of their rocky lives. Still, they didn't dwell on them. After a while, they'd turn to each other and say, *All right. That's done.* Max and Caroline would be home from work in an hour or two, so they had to make the most of their window of freedom. "Let's mix up a nice drink," Vivian would say. They'd pull the blinds, because they knew the neighbor would be watching. She was a fine old lady who made it her business to track the comings and goings in her pocket-size sphere of influence. Once they knew the coast was clear, Vivian and Willow would get a little toasty, crank up the surround sound, dance around the house, and wolf down marshmallows. They'd imagine the neighbor craning her neck, shaking her head, and muttering, *Oh, for the love of God*—all while making a mental note of what she'd later tell Max and Caroline. Vivian was never sure how much her dad and stepmom knew about those afternoons. By the time they got home, the girls had washed the glasses, put away the bottles, and straightened up the house. When the door opened, all that Max and Caroline saw were wide grins and angelic faces.

The fact was, Vivian avoided getting caught in pretty much every one of her youthful transgressions. She remained the dutiful daughter; the respectful, church-going girl; ever the hard worker; and the favored student at school. She also continued to cut herself, hiding the damage from everyone around her. And she began to have thoughts, terrible thoughts of pain and harm. They came as sharply drawn visualizations in waking hours, and hazy nightmares in sleep—placing her kitten in the dryer, pushing a boy who was mean to her down the stairs, or running someone over with a car. Each, in turn, horrified Vivian. She knew she would never commit such acts, but she couldn't shut the images down. *Go away, go away*, she would whisper. *Stop haunting me.* She convinced herself that she was the reason Max and Caroline couldn't have children—that God was punishing them for her intrusive thoughts. And she subtly loosened her ties to the most pristine aspects of her childhood, in part by drifting away from Josie.

Josie, meanwhile, wasn't particularly aware of Vivian's shift. True, the Bumble Bee Club had been dissolved, and their former club member Chloe had moved away when her dad had been called to serve a distant ministry. But Josie and Vivian continued to see each other at church, Sunday school and Vacation Bible School, and to play together occasionally outside their circle of faith. And Josie had become increasingly absorbed in her own routines of school, family life, and work.

Growing up, Josie knew her upbringing wasn't quite like that of most other Downeast kids. In front of her modest Cherryfield home, you wouldn't see an ATV, a staple of nearly every other driveway in these parts. You wouldn't find a gun in the house, and you wouldn't see the four Dekker girls out in the woods on Hunting Day with the rest of the neighborhood kids. Josie's maternal grandparents, Mae and Stuart, had settled in Cherryfield in the 1970s as "homesteaders," among the wave of out-of-staters with idealistic dreams of living off the land and soaking up the rural idyll of Maine. They tried to make a go of things by opening a farm, complete with dairy cows and blueberry fields, and raised Josie's mom, Brianna, and her two brothers while adjusting to the vicissitudes of Downeast life.

Homesteaders have dotted America's landscape for generations. In their original form, they were our nation's Western pioneers—the more than four million people who jumped at the chance, under the Homestead Act of 1862, to buy a 160-acre parcel of untouched public land for a pittance. Since that time, homesteading, even though no longer operating under that nineteenth-century legislation, has found its place as a lifestyle choice for Americans of every generation. It is a movement wrapped in self-reliance and independence, with agrarian ideals at its core. Life for back-to-the-landers, as they're commonly known, is often challenging, especially in a place like Maine—where short seasons and unpredictable weather can wreak havoc on the best-laid plans. The strongest and most enterprising Downeast homesteaders, like Mae and Stuart, are able to carve their own niche, and ultimately meld pre-homestead life experiences with adopted survival skills. In turn, their children, like Brianna and her brothers, grow up with a combination of Downeast sensibilities and exposure to other realms—and often find themselves dancing to a slightly different tune than that of their generationally rooted peers.

Indeed, when the time came for Brianna to graduate from Narraguagus, she didn't marry a high school sweetheart, and she didn't go straight to work. She went, instead, to college in Ohio. She wanted to study medicine, to be part of a world beyond her small hometown. And even though she loved her family with all her heart, she was certain she'd never return.

After college, Brianna interned at an environmental research institute in Michigan. There she met Dan, an engaging, creative Canadian, who had also recently finished college. They dated for a while, got married, and lived in Chicago for a year before moving to Canada. When their first daughter, Angela, turned one, Dan was diagnosed with a brain tumor. He fully recovered, except for the loss of hearing in one ear. But the experience was harrowing—and it stopped Brianna in her tracks. *What are we doing,* she asked, *raising our children so far from family?* When Brianna and Dan's second daughter, Elizabeth, was born, they packed up their belongings and headed south to Maine.

They chose to live on Great Cranberry Island, thirty miles south of Brianna's hometown of Cherryfield. Great Cranberry is the largest of five islands—known as the Cranberries—that sit off the coast of Mount Desert Island, just outside the confines of Acadia National Park. It's about two miles long and one mile wide, with a year-round population of forty. It was there that Josie was born. For a while, Dan taught in Great Cranberry's one-room schoolhouse. When school let out, he fished to make ends meet. The Dekkers didn't own a TV, so Dan and Brianna spent nights reading to their three young girls, and days admiring the magical sweep of Acadia's mountains across the open sea. In many ways it was a rewarding life. Still, it wasn't an easy—or quick—trip from Great Cranberry to Brianna's parents' home. And so, when Josie was two, the Dekkers packed up and moved to Cherryfield. Once there, Dan worked construction and put together enough savings to start a one-man roofing business. Not long after the birth of Katherine, the Dekkers' fourth and final child, Dan fell headlong off a roof. The brain damage he endured was temporary, but he couldn't speak for months. With the help of Brianna, who had gone back to school to study speech therapy, Dan fought his way back to normal brain function. Within a year he was on the job again.

Brianna would end up using her speech therapy training more than once in the Dekker household. As a toddler, Josie's speech was delayed, and once it came, she struggled to pronounce her words. "She was pretty hard to understand until she was five," recalled Brianna, who worked daily with Josie on her speech development from the time she was diagnosed. Mother and daughter also got help from Grammy Mae, who'd taken a job in early childhood education to help pay the bills that farming didn't cover. Mae had seen her share of preschoolers with challenges like Josie's, and worse. She knew that early interventions and consistent support made all the difference, and that too few local kids had either of these. Mae and Brianna counted their blessings as they took Josie by the hand. By kindergarten, she had pretty much kicked her affliction.

By the time Josie and her sisters were born, Grammy Mae and Pappy Stuart had sold their dairy cows. They'd turned their focus, instead, to selling square hay bales, and cultivating their long-standing blueberry business. They worked their two blueberry fields as a family, first with the help of a small crew of workers, then, when the price of blueberries began to bottom out and they couldn't turn a profit while paying for laborers, with the aid of a mechanical harvester. Every August, Josie would spend the bulk of her days on those fields. For the first five years of her life, Josie mostly sat and ate berries out of Dan and Brianna's buckets. But once she was strong enough to rake, it was up and at 'em at 6:00 a.m., and out in the fields until 4:00. It was, as Josie remembered, "hot and dusty, and full of spiders." When Grammy and Pappy moved to the harvester, Josie would still go in "and rake up the spots the harvester couldn't get." Season to season, Josie and her sisters did that farm work. They did whatever was needed, and knew enough not to complain too much. Hard work was a close third in Dekker values, just behind faith and family.

Indeed, as far back as Josie could remember, she and her sisters routinely pitched in with tasks beyond the farm. They mowed lawns at the handful of seasonal homes where Dan was caretaker to supplement the Dekkers' income. And when the girls were old enough to wield a hammer, each, in turn, worked construction alongside him.

As Josie grew, the Dekker name began to take on meaning around town. From the moment Mae and Stuart had arrived Downeast, they'd been determined not to retreat, as so many homesteaders did, when things got tough. They persevered, and within a few years, their new life had begun to take shape. In time, Mae and Stuart emerged as leaders at the Baptist Church. Mae taught Sunday school, organized auxiliaries, and ran benefit suppers whenever a community member was sick or injured. Dan and Brianna, meanwhile, had begun to establish their own identity, in part because of their daughters' successes at school. Teachers took note of the four captivating Dekker girls—each equally smart and motivated. So it was that through the daily living of their values, the Dekkers cultivated a worthy perch in Downeast life.

The secret of the Dekkers' success wasn't that those values placed them outside the Downeast norm. Indeed, the Dekkers' prioritization of family, faith, and work mirrored that of many of their neighbors. It was, instead, the Dekkers' attraction to less typical pursuits, and their deeply rooted engagement in education at home and beyond, that set Josie and her sisters on a different path—one that was bound to lead them far from Cherryfield and its environs.

There was, for starters, the way the Dekkers made reading a cornerstone of their daughters' lives—a necessity, really, almost like breathing. There was the near-constant presence of music in their home, the way it flowed through the fingers of every Dekker. Brianna played piano, Dan played guitar, and each of the girls was required to take at least one year of piano lessons, with hopes for more. Josie, for her part, began when she was five, and continued on through most of her high school years.

Then, too, there were the Dekkers' annual Christmas trips to Brockville, Ontario, where Josie's paternal grandparents showered the girls with Dutch culture and fare in a house devoid of internet and electronics. Josie grew to love those reunions—a "week of craziness" with nearly seventy Dekkers sprawled about the house that Josie's brickmason grandfather had built in the early 1970s. Time stood still in Grandma Liza and Grandpa Noah's Brockville home. Generations of Dekkers gathered to cross-country ski on trails behind the house, skate along the Rideau Canal, and play cards into the night. Teatime arrived punctually, twice daily at ten and two, with *boterkoek* and other Dutch treats stacked on carved china. And each year, as the family multiplied with kids and grandkids, they all returned. Josie would come to regard those gatherings as reruns of a classic old family film— timeless, innocent, and sweet.

As Josie looked upon the shape of her young life, she knew she was fortunate. Even though outsiders, and the government, would label the Dekkers low-income, her family was comfortable by Downeast Washington County standards. Dan and Brianna had steady work, with enough money to save a little along the way. Their girls had strong prospects for the future. Josie would later reflect that, as a family, they "were in a minority Downeast," both financially and structurally. "For instance," she observed, "my parents stayed together. They were strict, but I had constant support from them. There are a lot of kids who don't even know their biological parents, or if they do, they never see them."

When Josie was fourteen, she went on a weeklong, church-based missionary trip to the Dominican Republic. The poverty

Josie encountered was so pervasive that she couldn't fully grasp its magnitude. She returned Downeast overwhelmed by the suffering she'd seen, and inspired to go back. The following year, she made a second trip. But this time, when Josie arrived home, something changed inside her. She began to observe, as if for the first time, the long reach of poverty in Washington County. Classmates with no home to return to at night; coaches who routinely announced that students who couldn't afford a shirt or pair of cleats should see them privately; food pantries stationed at each of the local schools; students who barely bathed and wore the same clothes from one day to the next because they had no running water. How, she wondered, could this degree of distress be so extensive in her own hometown? And why had she been so blind to it before?

Chapter 5

Reverence

The catch was running high, and Mckenna was making quick work of her traps. It hadn't been long since she'd traded in her student fishing license for a commercial one. The license, which allowed Mckenna to double her trap load to three hundred, was a seventeenth birthday present from the state of Maine, and all Mckenna could think when she got it was, *It's about time.*

Mckenna's regular fishing territory—the Pleasant River— was actually an inlet that spilled into Pleasant Bay and out to the wide mouth of the Gulf of Maine. As Mckenna looked back from the bend of the river, the wharf—her wharf—began to disappear from sight. Beyond it, the sun crawled patiently upward, at war with the Downeast fog.

The *River Rodent* was a good boat, sturdy and reliable, even though it was a hand-me-down from Mckenna's older brothers, Dylan and Matthew. Mckenna had already set her sights on a newer, bigger boat, but she knew she'd have to wait until after graduation to pursue it. The simple truth was, if it were up to Mckenna, she'd be starting a full-time career in fishing as soon as school was out. But she'd made a promise to Phoebe and Jake that she'd get a college degree—a backup plan in case the lobster industry floundered. If she carried through with that promise, she'd be the first of the five in her family to earn a diploma beyond high school.

Mckenna rounded the river's inlet, slowed the *Rodent* to a near-dead stop, and pulled hard: once, twice, and over again. Country radio played in the background. Another sorrowful song of love gone awry. The pot hauler groaned, the ropes tightened, the trap tumbled onto the deck, and the lobsters came pouring out.

Four days a week in this, the summer before her Narraguagus senior year, Mckenna rolled out of bed at 6:00 a.m., grabbed her gear, and walked down the back driveway of her home to the family wharf. She often fished with her friend Isabel, the only other girl in her class who captained a lobster boat. Once the school year started, Mckenna would have to curtail her time on the water. Even so, she'd make sure to haul two or three times a week. She couldn't imagine what life would be like if she couldn't at least do that.

Despite her outward femininity, Mckenna was, in so many ways, like the male fishermen who came before her. She was as solid as steel, and utterly devoted to her craft. She stood in awe of the waters that allowed her to pursue that craft, even as she tried to tame them. She wrestled with gnashing waves when the winds picked up and she could barely hang on to the edges of her careening boat, and fought through the midsummer fog and rain in the hours before the sky would clear to reveal a glorious sun. She hauled traps well into November, wiping the frost from her deck as she braced herself against the bitter cold.

This day, as Mckenna continued to navigate the *Rodent*, she peered outward. At twenty-six feet, her boat handled the river well. But it wasn't made for the whims of the open sea. Mckenna knew from experience that Downeast weather, even within the river's confines, could turn on a dime. "You could start out with a crystal sky," she would say, "and once you're out there, the fog will close right in on you." At that point, there wasn't much you could do but trust your instruments and keep hauling.

Those instruments, combined with Mckenna's instinct, served her well. Between her GPS map and radar, she could monitor every one of her traps. With a glance at her screen, she knew the water depth beneath her and the distance to nearby boats. She could track the myriad dotted islands around her, even if she couldn't see more than three feet ahead.

Mckenna knew, too, that flying blind on a foggy day was not for the meek or unsteady. Then again, no one ever accused her of being either of those things. On the contrary—Mckenna was serenely confident, though never content. She knew she'd have to work longer, and harder, to upgrade to that bigger boat, but she had no doubt she'd get there. The Holts' four lobster boats, plus the wharf and the lobster pound that bore their family name, were a testament to the family's perseverance, and that testament had been inculcated in Mckenna. *You do what you love*, she had been taught from an early age. *You learn to do it right. And once you do, you've got to have the will to stick with it.*

When Mckenna had been out on the river the week before, the lobsters had held tight to their habitat, reminding her just how sharply their numbers controlled her fate. But today, the waters let loose a royal bounty, as if to reward her for not giving up.

She could hear her parents' lessons in her head as she hauled her final traps for the day, and glanced with satisfaction at all that she'd been able to reap. *Respect the work, and it will sustain you. Respect the waters, and they'll bring you what you need.*

True, the principles Phoebe and Jake had imbued in Mckenna didn't always hold sway. Mckenna couldn't quite muster up the will to work as hard in school as she did on her boat. It wasn't for lack of smarts—she had a quick mind, when she wanted to use it. She simply didn't care much for academics. She dutifully went to school and kept up with her classwork. She even earned good grades in most subjects, partly because her parents expected it of her, and partly because she was naturally competitive. But her heart wasn't in the books.

Mckenna knew that because she wasn't among the top four or five in her thirty-two-student class, some administrators and teachers would try to convince her to pursue a nurse's aide certificate. It's common practice at Narraguagus to steer students—especially girls—in that direction. Indeed, district leadership points with pride to the school's certified nursing assistant (CNA) program as an option that gives local girls the training they need to work in a nursing home or hospital right after graduation—and possibly, a path to a full nursing degree. There are plenty of CNA jobs to be had within commuting distance, and even though they pay little, they offer one of the few non-fishing avenues for stable, long-term employment.

As Mckenna moved through her high school years, well-meaning adults would say, *You really should get your CNA.* For a while, Mckenna would smile politely at them, and nod, with little intention of following their advice. Finally, she grew so tired of hearing about the benefits of the "CNA backup plan," she enrolled in the program and earned her certificate. "I didn't mind it," she would later say. "But I don't really care for school and I don't want to stress myself out to become a nurse if I'm never going to be one. It's not that I don't like working with people. I actually can enjoy it. I just don't like being strapped down."

After stopping to reflect, she explained a little more. "I've seen certain people go through nursing programs. They'll be super smart kids who are into the academic stuff. And they're still struggling to get by after they graduate." Their struggle wasn't easy for Mckenna to watch. It was even harder for her to imagine being in that position.

"Besides," she added, with a smile, "I just can't make myself sit down and read a book for very long. I can do it, but honestly, I'm not that interested. I'd much rather be out on my boat. Or if I'm going to sit down, I want to chill. I just want to watch TV."

But sports. That was another story. As a senior, Mckenna captained three of the school's most competitive varsity teams: soccer, basketball, and softball. She was a powerhouse in all three, but softball was Mckenna's true love. It was, perhaps, the only thing she placed on as high a pedestal as fishing. By junior year, Mckenna had already earned statewide recognition as a standout softball pitcher. She'd helped lead the squad to an undefeated season, with a heartbreaking near-miss in the Class C state championship semifinal game. This spring, she planned to finish the job.

Mckenna was known for her pitching speed and power. Her arm strength wowed the coaches and local fans. That strength was due, in no small part, to the daily routine of hauling lobster traps. Still, despite Mckenna's status as a star athlete, she often stood alone among her peers. If someone asked her if she was close with the girls in her class, she'd quickly respond, "Not anymore." She'd add, "They say stuff to me, they say stuff behind my back. They run me into the ground. But what it is, is just jealousy that I've put my time into pitching. I've worked hard to be where I am today. They didn't do it when they were younger, so they aren't where I am. And it bugs them."

She got along better with the boys, especially among the lobster-fishing crowd. But she showed little patience for the excuses they made for slacking at school and doing little more than fishing. "They'll say, 'Well, we're off fishing.' Well, I've been playing sports, and fishing, and keeping my grades up, all while you guys were just fishing." She knew she was competent, and she wasn't afraid to show it.

Indeed, Mckenna was a formidable seventeen-year-old. She loved her home, her family, and her boat. She venerated her country, her community, and her God. She didn't need to go to church to pray; she did it every day by bowing down to the gift of nature that sustained her way of life. She didn't need to talk about her faith with others; she expressed it with the gratitude for all that she reaped through hard work and discipline. She didn't need to talk about politics to show how much she valued being an American. She knew there were challenges in her own backyard, that things were far from perfect for too many families around her. But she wouldn't trade being exactly where she was for anything. And, quite frankly, she wasn't particularly interested in leaving—or someday, raising her own kids—in any other place than this. She had all she needed Downeast.

Some days, as Mckenna stood at the helm of her well-worn *River Rodent*, she'd stare intently at the water and sky before her. She'd think to herself how often she'd taken that view for granted. On those days, she'd fix her eyes on the majesty of the sunrise, the clusters of islands at every turn, and the miracle of a river so flat and calm that it practically dared you to dance on top of it. She'd think about the good fortune of being able to be her own boss, set her own hours, and work the days she wanted to work. She'd feel sorry for people who sat behind their desks and stared at computer screens all day long. She'd think, too, about the kids in her school whose families weren't connected to lobster fishing. Even if they were good workers, willing to give their all, she knew that most would never find a path to build the lives they deserved.

She'd gaze outward and say out loud, to no one in particular, "I've got to be the luckiest girl around."

Chapter 6

On the Horizon

While Mckenna fished, Willow lived that less fortunate life. She was determined to find a way out, but knew how steeply the odds were stacked against her. She was reminded daily of her lot in life by too many adults around her—by their reflexive frowns, and the way her name slid out of the sides of their mouths. *Newenham*, they would say. *Neewww-enn-hamm*, as if they were reaching into the cobwebs of their minds. *Oh yes. Oh. Right. Newenham.* Not much needed to be said after that, and little consideration needed to be given to the girl whose secrets weren't nearly as hidden as her parents had hoped they'd be.

Still, Willow clung to the hope that she could beat back her family's reputation. There had to be some adults—perhaps a kindhearted teacher or two—who would give her the shot she craved at becoming one of them. As she waited for that miracle, Willow found a respite by taking pictures of the natural beauty around her. The late-spring bloom of wild lupines, a violet and salmon mosaic of stalks that blanketed wide green fields. The morning fog that crept from the coastline inward and hovered like clotted cream well into the afternoon. The ice whose crystals refracted a thousand tiny beams of light to reveal a rainbow haze of possibility. Indeed, apart from hanging out with Vivian, peering through the lens of a camera was about the only thing that helped Willow through her toughest days.

And boy were there still plenty of those days. It seemed to Willow, in fact, that things were only getting worse. When she started seventh grade, her paternal grandmother, Sue, went to prison for embezzling more than thirty-five thousand dollars from the town while serving as its clerk. Willow recalled that her paternal grandfather, Francis, had been known for years around town as the "coke king." (As a child, Willow was confused by the name; she kept trying to figure out his connection to Coca-Cola.) Until about a year before her Grandma Sue was incarcerated, Willow hadn't been allowed to see either of them. But one day, she reached out. She was urged on by her maternal Grandma Ann, who had been her safe haven for so many years. Grandma Ann was a religious woman, strict but forgiving. She thought it was wrong to be strangers in a town so small.

For most of his adult life, Willow's dad hadn't spoken to his parents. Growing up, he and his brothers had been beaten so badly by their dad that one day the Maine Department of Health and Human Services took them away and sent them to live with their great aunt. When William was older, his mom stole his credit card and racked up thousands in debt. At thirty-six, he finally paid off most of it, thanks to the settlement from the Powell plant.

William had warned Willow to stay away from his parents, but she couldn't resist their lure. They had money. They offered to buy her things. They showered her with gifts. They had "two snowmobiles and a four-wheeler, and Grandpa Francis had two motorcycles for himself, a truck, a Mustang, an SUV, and the house." Then Grandma Sue got arrested, and the mystery of their riches was clarified.

While Grandma Sue served her time in prison, Grandpa Francis asked Willow to live with him. He'd never been on his own, and he needed someone to take care of him. "He said that if I was to live there, he would buy all my school clothes for the next year, and he'd take me wherever I needed to go." Willow wanted to get to know Grandpa Francis better. She thought the arrangement would be "awesome." So it came to be that at the start of summer between her seventh- and eighth-grade years, Willow moved in with her grandfather.

Once there, she saw the man her father knew. Grandpa Francis didn't beat her, but he "was very controlling. He had to have things a certain way. If I went into the grocery store and I got the wrong type of percentage for lean and fat for hamburger" he'd get angry, "and I needed to race back and get the right kind." He also became "paranoid of everything. He thought people were keying his vehicle, so he put up security cameras around the house and outside." Willow wasn't sure where his paranoia came from; she suspected it was "because of his long use of drugs."

Within weeks of Willow's arrival, her grandfather's house began to feel like another scary "family secret." Yet, even as Willow shrank from Grandpa Francis, she blamed Grandma Sue for what he had become. "She turned my grandfather into the monster that he is," said Willow. "He had his issues, but she amplified them." Willow's dad would later tell her that when he was young, it was his mom who "was always the reason us kids were getting beat." She would push and yell and instigate until his father couldn't bear it anymore—and the anger would move from her to him to each of the boys, until there was nothing left.

As Willow's summer drew to a close, she used the excuse of the start of school to flee her grandfather's house and move back in with her parents. Grandpa Francis was furious. He left a message on Willow's phone "swearing and telling me that I was the worst thing in the world." Nearly a year would pass before the two would speak again.

In January of Willow's eighth-grade year, Lily finally left William. She took her youngest, Isaac, and moved in with her new boyfriend in nearby Steuben. Willow stayed at Vivian's house for most of the remainder of the school year. There, she felt like a part of Vivian's family. Max and Caroline gave her a bedroom of her own, and showed her what it felt like to have parents who were present. They also enforced a strict set of rules. Yet, even while Vivian felt suffocated by their limits, Willow embraced them. She felt comforted to know that someone cared. Meanwhile, Willow's other brother, Scott, went to live with Grandma Ann. Lily had felt uneasy taking Scott with her to Steuben. He'd gotten too big and too angry, and Lily had grown too frightened of him.

With Willow's eighth-grade graduation came news that Grandma Sue was to be released from prison. That fall, upon Sue's return home, Willow again moved into her paternal grandparents' house. She'd had her heart set on attending Narraguagus High, but both her parents had moved out of the school district after their divorce. Sue and Francis's house was just down the road from Narraguagus; from there, Willow could walk to school each day. And so she returned, armed with the hope that this time things might be different.

During Willow's first two years of high school, she continued to live with Sue and Francis. In that time, she began to experience debilitating sinus infections. She found herself fighting off pain "nearly all the time, because I was draining myself, and I wasn't eating right and I wasn't sleeping right." Finally, Grandma Sue offered to take her to the doctor. As Willow stood at the registration desk, Sue tried to convince the receptionist to give her Willow's social security number. Willow panicked as she watched her grandmother work the staff member. It wasn't the first time Sue had pulled this trick; years earlier, she'd stolen money from her dad and uncle by using their social security numbers. When Willow got home from the doctor's office, she called her mom and told her what Grandma Sue had attempted—this time, unsuccessfully—to do. A few hours later, Lily arrived at the grandparents' house with her boyfriend and other family members as reinforcements. Willow's grandparents "had a gun in the house that wasn't under lock and key," a violation of Grandma Sue's parole, and a fact Willow had shared with her mom. Lily, recalled Willow, stood at the door and yelled, "If you don't let me in, I'll call the cops, and you won't like the repercussions."

A row ensued in the living room while Willow hid. Finally, Grandma Sue barged into Willow's room and "screamed and screamed and screamed." Willow quickly gathered what she could of her belongings and escaped with her rescuers, back to the safety of Grandma Ann's house. "We eventually got the majority of my stuff out," she remembered. "I still have a closetful down in their basement, and I haven't talked to them since."

Throughout those early Narraguagus years, Willow also struggled with fear and self-doubt. She was so shy that she "could barely speak to anyone." Her father, who had maintained joint custody of Willow and her brothers after the divorce, continued with his abuse of hydros. "You never knew," said Willow, how heavily he was using "until you saw him or spoke to him." As her freshman year wore on, Willow avoided her dad. She "couldn't stand to be near him," and would go months without speaking to him. Then, too, the damage William had done to Willow had infiltrated the choices she made with boys her age. Willow had started dating years earlier, back when she was in elementary school, and in nearly every instance, she'd gravitated toward boys who mistreated her. Only later would Willow connect the dots. "Growing up with a father who had that mental control over me," she'd say, "I never thought that I was worth anything. So I was always in a relationship with someone who demanded so much more of me than they should have."

At the end of her freshman year, Willow took a job at Sea Carnations Wharf in nearby Jonesport. Sea Carnations was one of the oldest lobster dealers in the nation, and in high season, it was a hub of activity. Willow had gotten to know the wharf through her dad, who for years had worked there intermittently as a dock hand.

It was also at that time that Willow's brothers had clamored to live with their dad for the summer. But Willow didn't trust William, and she wasn't about to let Scott and Isaac spend two months alone with him. So she joined them. Not long after the three kids moved in with their dad and his girlfriend, Willow learned just how sharp her instincts were. For this was the summer that she watched William descend from hydros to heroin. "For a while," recalled Willow, "he kept saying, 'No, no, no. I'm not gonna do that.' Then one day he was like, 'Yeah, okay, I'll do it.'" There sat Willow and her brothers, together at Dad's house in Jonesport, with the anger and the girlfriend and the heroin, and no way out. And through those weeks, the only thing that kept Willow going was the daily call of her duties at the wharf.

When school resumed in the fall, Willow began to have

dreams so terrifying that they'd jolt her awake in a cold sweat: nightmares of her dad chasing and beating her. She realized that unless she sought help, she'd never free herself of her family history. "I finally came into school and said, 'I need to see a therapist.' I was worried that I was like my father, that I was bipolar and paranoid. But I learned, instead, that I just had severe anxiety, severe depression, and a lot of trust issues." Willow felt fortunate to be able to get help at Narraguagus; she had neither the access to nor funds to pay for a private therapist outside of school. That spring, Willow also worked up the courage to try her hand at managing the girls' varsity softball team. She saw it as a way to escape from her home life, "to have something different." She liked it so much that she signed up to manage the girls' volleyball and girls' and boys' basketball squads as well.

As time passed, Willow's high school experience started to come together. She found camaraderie through sports, and earned solid grades in her classes. She began to trust a handful of adults—particularly her art teacher, Britt Frances, and the school's softball coach and phys ed teacher. She saw in them the honesty and encouragement she'd longed for since childhood. She opened up to the girls on the teams she managed. They embraced her, and helped her "through more than one bad relationship." And she, in turn, nurtured and supported them—often acting as a go-between to the coaches when a teammate struggled on the field or court "because she was having family issues, or had just lost a relative." She pulled them close, and called them her ducklings. And she began to heal.

As Willow wound her way through her Narraguagus years, she continued to work at the wharf. At first, she spent most of her time on the docks, helping the fishermen with manual tasks. She picked up hours whenever she could—after school, on weekends, and in summer months, when the wharf was practically overrun with lobster boats. She worked hard and proved her value to the bosses there—so much so that after a while she landed an office role, as an assistant to the wharf's secretary.

Willow came to love that wharf, and the grandeur of the sea that spilled outward from its hulking, weather-beaten docks. There, she was able to share in the fellowship of fishermen, who checked in with her regularly to tally up their lobster hauls and get paid. She joked with them, spoiled them, and found comfort in their hard-edged routines. She also began to gain a sense of what sustained her. She felt the depth of her reverence for the vast ocean before her—for all the possibilities it embodied— and her respect for the fishermen who toiled in it. These fishermen filled her heart. The sea they roamed became the backdrop for her dreams. This wharf, and the sense of purpose it allowed her to feel, began to shape the contours of her budding life.

As soon as she could drive, Willow developed a nighttime routine that stood in sharp contrast to her chaotic life. She would slip out of whatever place she happened to temporarily call home, and steal away to Sea Carnations Wharf in the dark of night. She'd arrive well after the final haul of the day had been brought in, and well before the predawn boats set out for the farthest reaches of Maine's lobster territory. There she would stretch her body across the massive dock's bobbing planks, and stare outward to the vague and unreachable horizon. Whether at night, when alone, or during the day, when surrounded by fishermen, Willow knew that this was the place she could find peace with herself and the world around her. It was her refuge, and her church—and each time she made her way to it, she whispered a silent prayer of gratitude for what she had found.

Part Two

Dilemmas

Chapter 7

The Game Changers

Words echo across the halls of Narraguagus High. Groups form vaguely in the usual places: the jocks, the nerds, the artists, the lobster-fishing crew, and the handful of migrant and immigrant kids, whose parents were drawn Downeast by seasonal work. Together, they form an adolescent symphony, part playful, part hopeful, part wicked, part flickering with insecurity. Calls for help echo too, from kids whose childhoods have been stolen.

Nearby, the teachers strain to look like they're not listening. But they hear.

Jim Swenson spent a lot of time thinking about those kids, especially the sons and daughters of the opioid addicted. It was April, a few months before Jim's retirement from Narraguagus High. When he wasn't at the high school, juggling the roles of assistant principal and athletic director, he was out on the water, lobster fishing. Or operating a seasonal restaurant four towns over with his wife. Or teaching diving and underwater archaeology an hour's drive from the restaurant, at the University of Maine at Machias. There were plenty of others around here like Jim, neighbors who stretched themselves across multiple jobs—each of which, by most accounts, would be considered full time.

That's just how life was Downeast. How it had always been. There weren't enough hours in the day to do what was needed—to scratch up steady money to keep the bills paid, make sure the kids were fed, and still have a little something left to keep your truck running smooth and looking new.

For Jim, the work helped with all those things. But each job was also a labor of love. He knew he was among the fortunate. Assistant principal at Narraguagus was a top job, one he'd earned after seventeen years of teaching at the school. Being able to fish and dive helped him keep his sanity. And owning a restaurant—one that sat on the edge of the Mount Desert Narrows and enticed tourists exploring Acadia—well, that was a godsend.

By looks, Jim was every bit the rough-edged Mainer. He had a round, ruddy face, with warm creases etched across a broad forehead. When he spoke, his Downeast accent flooded the room. Vowels stretched and lingered. Consonants scampered to dusty corners before they could be properly identified. But today, as sharp spring winds forced nearby spruces to tremble, Jim Swenson's voice hung softly. "I promise you this," he said, "I don't believe a day goes by when we don't see crying: boys, one a day; girls, three or four a day. Every one of them is struggling with turmoil at home. And it's always fentanyl, always drugs."

Lauren Donovan nodded her head in agreement. The slender Narraguagus principal had just rejoined Jim in her office. As she sat, the intercom on her desk buzzed, and she darted off again, to tackle the latest disruption. Most days, it seemed, that buzzer never stopped. When, moments later, Lauren returned, she gazed wistfully outward and ran her fingers through her neatly layered bob. Things hadn't always been this way.

Lauren and Jim had worked as a team at Narraguagus for three years. They'd found their rhythm quickly, despite their contrasting personalities—Jim's gruffness juxtaposed with Lauren's light touch. Some said Lauren's touch was too light. *You give 'em an inch*, they'd murmur, *and . . . you know the rest.* They'd shake their heads and reminisce about a time when you could give those kids a little old-fashioned you-know-what. But Lauren knew what lay behind the mask of the school's most audacious kids. She understood.

Indeed, Lauren had grown up with most of their grandparents. She'd watched their parents come of age, taught them in her own classroom, and seen them slip into the cycle lived by generations that preceded them. She had held a good number of these very kids as babies, and smiled as her own grandkids grew up beside them. They were known to her, and she to them, in an intricate pattern not easily unraveled.

Lauren herself had graduated from Narraguagus more than forty years earlier. She was the direct descendant of Cherryfield's Revolutionary-era founder—and she was one of dozens of deeply rooted Cherryfield Donovans who'd made their way through those doors. Hard to believe, she'd think, it had been that long. In that time, Lauren had watched the challenges of her hometown escalate. She'd witnessed it here, every day, at the high school. Too many kids "coming in angry, acting out." Flailing, as though they'd been swept up by a storm surge. And in nearly every instance, she and Jim would learn that a parent had OD'd, or had been arrested, the night before. Or fists had flown, doors had slammed, and voices had risen so high and fast they'd surely have woken the neighbors, if only their homes had been set a little closer. The kids came and went, and Lauren and Jim did what they could. They used the limited targeted resources the school had, and turned to others—teachers, coaches, churches, and families who had more—to keep those kids safe, and learning, through it all.

Along the way, Lauren had also witnessed something that some might call unexpected. The way, in this seemingly male-dominated culture, that local girls were kicking ass. Year after year, they rose to the top. They were, Lauren observed, the leaders. The really good athletes. Dominating academically, and taking top honors in science and math. Finding their way into medical fields and engineering. Or, like Mckenna and Audrey, fishing from an early age—and making good money at it—while still putting in the time and effort to do well in school. These girls gave Lauren the strength to keep pushing. Every day, as that intercom buzzer sounded again, she rooted for them.

And what of the boys? Far too many weren't anywhere near what they could be. "You'll see them with hoods up, and it's almost like they're trying to hide," said Lauren. "Like they've given up." Then, the boys who are fishermen, "they go out on the boat and work their butts off all day long, but they can't get themselves wrapped around schoolwork for anything." Lauren had seen it time and again. Too few boys stepping forward—in academics, in sports, in ways that might show other boys that more was possible. She knew they weren't the only ones. She'd talk to administrators in schools across the region, and they'd nod their heads in agreement and throw up their hands and say, *What can we do?* She'd look at the Narraguagus class ranking and sigh. Two years running, only one in the top eight was a boy, with pretty much the same trend every year prior that Lauren could recall. She'd look back to the annual regional conference basketball awards—honors that made the Downeast locals stop and cheer—and nearly all had gone to girls. To be sure, there were boys who excelled. One, a distant relative of Lauren's, was poised to share valedictorian honors with Josie later that year, and would go on to enroll at Bowdoin College in the fall. Audrey's oldest brother graduated top of his class from the Maine Maritime Academy with a degree in engineering before returning home to fish full time. Significant numbers of boys went on to serve their country in the military, and this, too, was a particular point of pride for the community.

Still, it seemed to Lauren that many of the boys "feel as though they can't do anything right, no matter what they say or do. Sometimes," she added, "I wonder if we've gone too far in disempowering the boys. If we're pushing our boys backward. In this school we have almost exactly half and half girls and boys, but if you look at the kids that float through this office every day, it's the boys. I have one or two girls that I can pretty much guess I'll see on a regular basis, but that's it, out of a hundred and fifty girls." There was, thought Lauren, "a kind of batting down among the boys that goes on, that constant feeling like everything they say and do is wrong. And maybe that's why they're not trying. Someone needs to show them the way, without making it seem as though they are being put down all the time."

Each year, Lauren tried hard to rally folks behind the handful of boys who showed potential. She searched for male role models, and sought guidance from those who'd walked a rocky path and come out the other side. It wasn't easy, but she found a few. One was a former Harvard football coach named Manny Parsons, who'd arrived in Cherryfield in 2002 to develop and run Downeast Washington County's only comprehensive youth program.

Manny grew up on the edge of Boston. He was a working-class kid, the sort whose combination of natural smarts and athletic ease turned heads. By the time Manny had entered high school, he'd caught the eye of more than one college football coach. He landed a full scholarship at Wichita State and headed west, a first-generation college student. Before traveling to Kansas his freshman year, Manny had left his home state only once before, for a high school football trip to Florida. On the field, Manny showed enough promise that the Pittsburgh Steelers drafted him. Off the field, he developed a passion for helping kids. Manny never did end up playing pro ball, though. He and his high school sweetheart, Lois, instead joined the Peace Corps and headed off to the Philippines. They were young, newly married, and eager to serve. When the pair returned to the States, Manny spent a decade teaching middle and high schoolers in the Boston area, while coaching football at Harvard. Then, one day, Manny and Lois packed up their belongings, piled their kids in the car, and headed to midcoast Maine. They wanted to develop a youth program there, to do something more for kids who had less. And they did.

A few years later, a call came from the highly regarded Bar Harbor–based Maine Seacoast Mission. The mission was offering Manny and Lois the chance to start a well-funded program in Washington County, to give local kids the kind of structured in-school, after-school, and summer experiences that had long been commonplace in better-heeled areas. The mission named the effort EdGE, in memory of Ed Greaves, a part-time Addison resident and mission board president who had long pushed to bring Downeast's kids more hands-on learning—the kinds of experiences that would build skills, character, and leadership. With the EdGE program infused with generous funding from a dear friend of Greaves, and Manny and Lois at the helm, Greaves's hopes, albeit posthumously, were on the verge of being realized.

Still, it wouldn't be an easy task. When Manny and Lois arrived in 2002, most locals were skeptical. They'd seen their share of nonprofits swing through these parts. Cadres of well-intentioned out-of-towners would arrive, armed with Power-Point presentations and just enough funding to last a year or two before they'd have to start scratching around for more to keep their promises alive. Most were gone before anyone could recall what it was they were trying to do.

Manny remembered that feeling, the sense that the locals were waiting for him and Lois to pack it up, the collective shrug that greeted them. He couldn't say he blamed them, either; he knew what they'd encountered time and again. But he and Lois kept at it, and hoped their efforts might bring a little more joy to Downeast's kids, a little more peace of mind to parents and grandparents who worked long hours and could not be there for their kids each afternoon.

It was slow work, at times painstaking, to convince the locals that the Seacoast Mission was committed for the long term. "It took us five years," said Manny. "It didn't really come until we put up the EdGE building in Cherryfield. They saw that structure going up, and finally said, 'I think they're here to stay.' Until then, every year, I'd go into a local administrative team meeting, and someone would say, 'Manny, you leaving this year?'" But in the end, Manny and Lois convinced the community they had what it took to make it Downeast. They'd also had the foresight not to venture here without the kind of backing that would last a good long while. Manny and Lois had no desire to spend their time chasing grants when they could be outside with the kids, showing them what it felt like to find adventure in their own glorious backyard, and to learn from it.

Manny and his staff knew, too, that they needed to make it easy for parents and kids to turn to EdGE. "Everything is so spread out. I've got to go ten miles for a Coke. That's a twenty-mile round trip. I better damn well need something pretty badly before I want to use a tank of gas to go to the store. Some of these kids, they live way out there, twenty, twenty-five miles away. As a family, are you gonna go fifty miles here and back to take your kids to the EdGE building? I don't think so. So we put in free busing. Worked our hours around their schedules, and used the schools as program sites. Everything that might make it hard to participate, we eliminated it."

And when EdGE came calling, the kids showed up, first in trickles, then in waves, until there were eight hundred of them riding the mission's buses every year. Manny taught these kids to find purpose in their ruggedness. He knew the boys, especially, needed to be encouraged. Girls like Josie and Vivian and Audrey, all of whom had spent time at EdGE as mentors, were self-motivated. They'd emerge as leaders, no matter what challenges he'd set before them.

But the boys—Manny and the EdGE staff took extra pains to push and pull and pile them into those mission buses so they could see what lay beyond the Downeast shores. Few of them had ever been past Bangor, so EdGE set up day trips to Portland and Orono, and overnights to Boston, Providence, New York, and Washington, D.C. "A lot of them would laugh, because they'd be going through a toll for the first time. Many of them have never ridden an escalator, never been on an elevator. Once, when we were crossing the Tobin Bridge into Boston, one of the boys yelled 'Where is the Statue of Liberty?' I told him they'd moved it to New York."

Manny opened these kids' eyes to possibilities, even if they would decide never to leave Downeast again. "What I want for them," said Manny, "is to have that ability to work as a team, to take on challenges with critical and creative thought. To be able to see the big picture and work well in their communities. So whether it be a Select Board, planning board, school committee, or anything like that, they can work together, and maybe even lead the way."

Manny gave them that, and more. There were setbacks, to be sure, and holes in kids' hearts so big that no amount of care could ever mend them. But by the time Manny retired, nearly twenty years after he and Lois had arrived Downeast, he knew their labors had not been for naught. EdGE had become a local household name—with a twelve-million-dollar endowment facilitated by the Maine Seacoast Mission to bolster it. What's more, the mission had expanded its local reach well beyond its focus on kids. Alongside the EdGE building, on a slice of Cherryfield land robust enough to be dubbed a campus, Lois now oversaw a full sweep of mission services for local families: a food pantry, a weekly Table of Plenty, a fully loaded community center, and a housing rehab effort that welcomed hundreds of volunteers a year from churches and community groups across the country. There was no question in anyone's mind, the Seacoast Mission had arrived. And it *was* here to stay.

Back in Lauren's office, the intercom buzzed one last time, and the end-of-day bell rang loud and long through the Narraguagus halls. It was, for most, a happy sound—the sound of bounding out to the playing fields, or onto nearby fishing boats, or five miles down the road to EdGE for a brief sojourn. But not for all.

The kids who were left lingered with nowhere in particular to go. "Lauren and I have cried," said Jim, "when we've seen what some of our kids go through. It's overwhelming." The pair had been around long enough to know that some people, including a handful of local school board members, thought it wasn't the job of the school and its teachers to take those students under their wing. To do "all the things that families used to do. Well," said Jim, sweeping his arms outward as if to reveal the breadth of the task they faced, "maybe we don't want it to be. But it is."

Chapter 8

Frannie

There was something about Downeast Washington County that
drew her to it—made Britt Frances pack her belongings at age
fifty-two and drive clear across the country to live there. Maybe
it was her longing for a quieter life, a break from the frenetic
pace in Bay Area California. Maybe it was the images of pristine waterfront properties her husband, Luke, had found while
browsing real estate websites; the swaths of green pressed alongside alluring waterscapes, despite the fact that neither had ever
set foot in Maine. Maybe it was the tug Britt felt each time she
stepped past the Washington County–made table that sat in her
home. More than half a century had gone by since her parents,
honeymooning across Maine, had decided they had to have that
table. Less than a year had passed since they—first her mom,
and shortly thereafter her dad—had left this earth.

Whatever the reasons, in the summer of 2007, Britt and Luke
found themselves pulling up to their new home in Addison,
Maine. The nearly 100-acre site, which Luke had found through
a solo house-hunting expedition ten months earlier, was a former

camp. Britt was no stranger to captivating locations; she had lived in New York, Switzerland, California, and Oregon. But as she caught sight of the place she would now call home, she gasped. "It's gorgeous," she thought to herself. "Perhaps the most gorgeous place on earth." And she knew that Downeast Maine was where she was meant to be.

By forty-five, Britt had pretty much everything she could ask for: a well-respected career as a graphic designer, a loving husband, nearby family, and a solid routine. But technology had begun to reshape the field of computer graphics, and Britt, in response, went back to school to keep up with the new terrain. She also began to think about options for another line of work. She earned her teaching credential and soon found herself teaching a range of subjects at a local East Bay high school. The school was part of a sprawling district that had its share of disadvantaged kids. It also housed a highly rated arts academy, in which Britt found the role she valued most, teaching art.

Britt knew that working at the academy was a "cherry assignment. Yes, we saw a few kids who dropped out. Yes, we had all kinds of social problems, but overall," said Britt, "the success was unbelievable." She stayed for six years. Then Maine beckoned, and Britt took the only available job opening at Narraguagus High: as a substitute teacher. Soon, she and Luke found themselves setting up a homestead Downeast, feeling like they'd landed on a new frontier.

A few months after the Franceses' eastward roll of the dice, Narraguagus High's longtime art teacher retired, and Britt got the job she'd coveted. Despite the fact that she was now a permanent member of the school roster, Britt worried that the community would never fully embrace her. And yet, she needn't have. At nearly every turn, she witnessed the locals' depth of heart—toward her, and so many others. It wound its way in and out of people's homes, in tins and baskets and offers to cut and carry and mend and grow whatever might help a neighbor get by. It came at a pace and frequency Britt had not encountered before she'd moved Downeast. "What was most amazing to me," she said, "was the number of benefit suppers to support students that have gotten sick, siblings that have gotten hurt or wounded, families that have faced an acute hardship. Everybody comes, and they drop a lot of money, and sometimes they don't even eat." Before long, the Franceses found themselves full force on the supper circuit. "Every week there was a different one. I finally told Luke, I can't do it anymore. We're eating so fast, and not even chewing, and even though we're full, we're waiting for that pie." Still, they kept going. For these were the rituals—the uncomplicated gestures and unspoken bonds that came with simply being there—that allowed Britt to begin to understand the culture of her adopted home.

In turn, Britt offered her students her lens—on art and life. Pretty much every local kid would pass through the Narraguagus art room doors at some point. They had to if they wanted to graduate. Some came with eager gaits and curious eyes. Most dragged their backpacks, loud and low. They faced Britt with their broad shoulders, toned from the labors they'd always known. They slid onto metal stools, rested their elbows on paint-pocked drafting tables, and peered at her with open stares, as if to say, *What is it you expect of me?*

Quite a lot, as it turned out. This wholehearted artist, with a laugh that could melt ice and a wit that could slice through the deepest Downeast fog, had somehow landed on the shores of Maine's northern coast, and now revealed wonders that rivaled even the most glorious seascapes they'd witnessed since birth.

She took these kids of lobstermen and farmers and blueberry rakers, of nurse's aides who'd married too young and hoped too much—and she showed them what it meant to dream in color. Then she pushed them to dream bolder, until their minds were filled with so many lines and hues that they had no choice but to spill a sliver of them onto the canvas that sat patiently before them.

And she found that these third- and fourth- and fifth-generation children of Downeast shared hopes and experiences well beyond what she'd ever anticipated.

And then. Well, then Britt Frances took the artwork of these kids, who too often deemed themselves unworthy, and she hung it in a gallery in Milbridge. Maybe, until that moment, they'd thought their efforts didn't measure up. But they had worked hard in this class and they'd finally looked up with hope in their eyes. At which point, Britt had nodded, with a smile, and quietly said, "I love it."

It was through that work, and through those eyes, that Britt had absorbed the contours of Downeast life. Coming into it, she hadn't expected to be surprised. "We had some of the same kind of stuff going on at Valley High—single parents, one parent married multiple times, heart-wrenching abuses. But something was different here—when you met someone, you met a history. You met so-and-so. Who was so-and-so. And then was married to so-and-so, the daughter of so-and-so. You'd listen, and you'd try to follow it all, until you'd finally put up your hands and say, '*Whoa whoa whoa. Hold on.*' But that," said Britt, "is the Downeast story. The family story that defines who these kids are."

Back in California, one of Britt's master's program teachers, who knew Washington County well, had warned her to do her due diligence before moving there. "He told me it wouldn't be easy," said Britt. "That it has one of the highest percentages of generational poverty in the nation. But I just thought, 'Oh, I can deal with poverty.' I'd seen poverty in California. I'd worked with kids who didn't have much. In my own life, my dad had lost jobs, and we'd had times when we had no money. To this day, Luke and I struggle for money. But then I saw it: the child abuse, the sexual abuse, the kids who don't have enough to eat at home. The parents who come to parent-teacher night and, when they smile and say hello, you realize they have hardly any teeth. I saw all this, and I knew. This, here, is *whole poverty*. Not situational poverty, but generational poverty."

Britt saw, too, that hardship did not confine itself to multi-generational Downeast families. It extended to migrant families who arrived, each season, from Central and South America, and from Mexico. Some of these families came by way of southern farms, where they'd stopped for winter work before heading north to Maine's warm-weather harvests. Bit by bit, they'd make their way. First a father, or an uncle, or a sturdy cousin who'd recently come of age. Then mothers, aunts, and grandparents, pressing the little ones against their weary bodies, whispering soft words as they tried to imagine what lay ahead. When the families finally reunited Downeast, they'd stand side by side in the work that would sustain them through the fall. They'd take in the breadth of the blueberry barrens whose bounty would help feed and clothe their children, even as those children toiled with them. From time to time, when the burden felt too heavy to bear, they'd straighten their backs and lift their eyes upward. And they would imagine a time when they might no longer be tethered to the tilt of the earth as it circled the scorching sun.

Each year, as August drew to a close, the children of migrant workers would arrive at Downeast's schools, only to leave by winter's frost. There were, at Narraguagus, only a handful in each class. They made their way, quietly and purposefully, carrying the burden of privation while trying not to reveal its weight. But life was hard, and pleasures were scarce. And if Britt, or any other teacher, ever needed a reminder of these hardships, she would not have to search for long.

On one occasion, Britt assigned her class a photo sequence, and through it, gained a window into one migrant student's reality. The boy had chosen to photograph a simple subject—a family member drinking a beverage. In the background, blurred, Britt could tell "there was no table in the room. There was one chair. You could see that the family lived there, but the place was bare." Soon after, when the school's English as a Second Language teacher put out a call for furniture for another migrant student's family, it would become clear that this boy's circumstances were not uncommon. "We had all this perfectly good extra stuff lying around," said Britt, "so Luke and I went to deliver it. You couldn't see it from the outside, but an entire family was living in one room, with nothing to sleep on but a few easy chairs."

It might have been easiest for children with lives so transitory and barriers so monumental—whose parents' education rarely went beyond fourth grade—to throw up their hands and say "I can't." But they didn't. Instead, they carried with them the aspirations their parents had instilled in them, and worked as though their future depended on their every action. Because it did.

Britt witnessed all this, and more, from her art room in the far corner of Narraguagus High. Among migrant families, too many kids for whom the pleasures of childhood peaked too early. Among multigenerational families, too many "kids raising themselves, whether it's because their moms and dads had children too young and didn't know how to be a parent, or because of alcohol or drug abuse, or depression." She saw, in the most vulnerable, too few instances of "kids just being kids."

She saw, especially among the multigenerational set, "a lot of girls with sexual partners at a really young age." Britt was aghast early on when a ninth-grade girl mentioned that her parents had allowed her to spend the night at her boyfriend's house. Britt relayed her concerns to a colleague with Downeast roots. "Well," responded the teacher, matter-of-factly, "you know the boy she's seeing is a so-and-so." A boy from an established family. "It was like a trophy," Britt recalled, "and if that girl was to get pregnant and marry into that family, even if things didn't work, that was okay." Britt paused. "That's not parenting, if you ask me. But it is part of the culture. If the pool is really small, and you have nothing, you see it as a strategy, a way to get ahead."

Still, no matter how tough the circumstances of her students, Britt would not lie to them, even if a lie might make things seem, just for the moment, a little easier. And she, in turn, would say to them, "You never need to lie to me, because it's really hard to come back from a lie." She talked honestly with them. She laughed honestly with them. She treated them like they were her own. And she let them know she would help them with whatever they needed. "I'll let them know they can call me at three o'clock in the morning, rather than have them get in the car with someone who's drunk or stoned. I'll tell them, 'I'm not going to give you a lecture. I may not be smiling at you when I pick you up, and I'll probably look like hell, but do not throw your life away.'" She paused, and reflected. "The phone rang this morning at six fifteen," she said. "At six fifteen you think, 'Oh no!' It was one of my former students. She started a new job yesterday, and she has to get up at three o'clock for it. She got on the phone and said, 'I knew you'd be up.' She'd called to tell me that she loved me."

For a handful of students each year, most often girls, the connection to Britt straddled teacher and friend. One by one, these girls found Britt, and began to open up to her. So it was for Vivian, and, in turn, for Josie and Willow—all of whom first met Britt as freshmen, and returned to study with her each of their remaining Narraguagus years. Each girl was drawn to the art room in ways particular to her passion: for Vivian, through her writing; for Josie, through drawing and sculpture; and for Willow, through the clarity of purpose that she discovered behind the camera lens.

For Vivian—as for Willow—Britt would often take on a parental role. "I'm biased," Vivian would say, "because I love her. But I think she is the most objective thinker at Narraguagus. She sees things from an outside point of view, but she's also able to put herself in a student's shoes, whatever our circumstances. She's seen a ton of kids go through her art room doors, and she's been close with so many students who've come from nothing, absolutely nothing. She knows how tied we are to our community, how loyal we are. But she also knows a lot of us want to get away, even just for a while. With me, she knows I want to be home with all my heart, but I don't. She sees that tension. And she makes it okay to feel that way."

For Josie, whose relationship with her parents was rock solid, Britt would emerge as a combination of sounding board and adult friend. She was, recalled Josie, someone "I could talk to without the feeling of 'Oh, no, I'm disappointing my parents.' I could turn to her for advice." Josie recognized that rare ability in Britt to balance being a teacher and a friend. "She is an old soul," said Josie, "but also a really young one in the same body. She understands kids and knows when it's time to tell you you're being stupid, to get a grip. She also knows when it's time to just give you a hug. I remember one day, I had just broken up with my boyfriend. I walked into her class and she immediately said, 'You're not okay.' And I responded 'No, no, I'm fine.' When class ended, she said, 'Josie, come back here. You've got a frog in your throat the size of an apple.' She gave me a hug, and I just started sobbing. Moments like that are the ones I'll always remember— where she knew me well enough to know when I was not okay."

The girls called her Frannie, and she, in turn, came to regard them as the children she'd never had. She allowed them to recount details of their lives that, in those moments, had cast a veil of darkness over them. She allowed Vivian to uncover her razor's-edge scars and reveal an adolescence stitched together by familial strife. She allowed Josie and Vivian, together, to wonder out loud about the presence of a God who would bring suffering into the world, and the seeming ease with which the church of their childhood would bat away their uncertainty. She allowed Willow to slowly and gingerly unpack her layers of pain, to share the family secrets that had bound her up so tightly she could barely breathe.

Most of all, she allowed them to ask, *What if?*

Chapter 9

Half-hearted Tragedy

When Vivian arrived at Narraguagus High, she was, outwardly, a part of it all. She played on the freshman softball team, dated the most popular guy, and ran with the coolest kids. She was, in Willow's words, "a social butterfly." Now, at fourteen, she'd plunged into a full-on courtship with recklessness. Vivian knew that her dad—and especially her stepmom, whose faith-bound rules had tightened the reins in the Westford household—wouldn't approve of her antics, of the drinking, the pot smoking, the "getting around" with boys. She didn't want to disappoint them—or her mom, in whom she confided more of her transgressions. But Vivian also knew this: she was cute; she was popular; she didn't have anything to tie her down; and she was hurting inside.

So she went on, earning praise for her intelligence and dedication at school and church, then sneaking off to rebel against the very tenets that she appeared to embrace. She'd go down to the lake with her boyfriend of the moment, one of a succession of "charming, but emotionally damaged" boys she'd dated through her middle and high school years. Once, Vivian nearly drowned.

She'd gotten drunk and had tried to swim naked across the lake to a nearby island. The episode didn't faze her much. She felt invincible, impervious to the threat of injury, or worse. She'd sneak out of her house in the dead of night. She'd breathe in the crisp night air and grab on to that momentary perfection—of feeling totally and completely unbound. Sometimes, she'd run down the road to her friend Brent's, crawl through his bedroom window, and find in him a willing friend for a night of folly.

One night, they took a four-wheeler out onto the slice of the Sunrise Trail that ran directly behind their houses. They rode all the way to Columbia, three towns over, and stayed in a tent behind her boyfriend Tommy's house. Tommy was among the boys whom Vivian's dad had forbidden her to see. He was "sweet and artistic, and really bad news." Vivian headed home early the next morning feeling light and free as a hummingbird in spring. When she tiptoed inside, the house was quiet and about as frigid as the inside of an ice hut. Vivian had left the door unlocked and the wind had blown it open while she'd been gone. She thought to herself, *I've done it this time*, and waited for her dad and stepmom to awaken and call her out. But they didn't. Perhaps they recognized her need to exhale and chose to ignore it. Perhaps they didn't know what to do. Regardless, she was simply grateful to be spared.

Willow, on the other hand, was fully aware of every one of Vivian's antics, particularly during the time she lived with the Westfords, in those months following her own parents' divorce. But she rarely participated. She recognized the magnitude of Max and Caroline's generosity, and she wasn't about to screw things up.

So it was that, as Vivian danced on flames, Willow held back— and regularly counseled her best friend to be more careful. She was, in Vivian's words, like "an old lady, the kind you couldn't help but love." She knew what danger looked like and felt no need to chase it. She wanted to protect Vivian, to remind her that, even though her life was imperfect, she had everything a girl could want. The indissoluble love of not two, but three parents. A structure on which to scaffold dreams. The warmth of family dinners and the sturdy pleasures of working together out back at the bait shop, or off on the Westford farm. A well of laughter and tears that didn't end with screams and sirens.

Indeed, Willow regularly recognized the irony of the two girls' adolescent roles: that she—the girl without a home, the one whose family bore a permanent stain—hewed to caution, while Vivian partied her nights away. Through it all, Willow saw what Vivian could not—the irreplaceable value of having a home with parents who cared too much. "There was so much love at Vivian's house. Yes, her parents were strict. She wasn't allowed to swear. There wasn't any alcohol. But it was just like what I imagined a home could be. And then you had my family, all about swearing and alcohol and everything. And it's funny, because the way Vivian and I acted, you'd think we'd grown up in each other's houses."

As time passed, Vivian began to realize that she couldn't sustain the pace of her under-the-radar activities; that whatever it was she was trying to find wasn't out among the weeds on the moonlit Sunrise Trail. She started to see a therapist in Ellsworth twice a week. She also, increasingly, found a release through the written word, and learned to use it to come to terms with her depression. In her earliest teenage years, Vivian had written only for herself, with the encouragement of her mother. Now, she began to open her voice to others, through the mentorship of Britt Frances, who would become her confidante.

As a freshman, Vivian had shown such artistic promise that, in her second year, she'd been invited to enroll in Advanced Art. There, she would be joined by Josie and Willow, who'd also emerged as early talents. When they gathered in Britt's art room, eager to live up to the honor of their selection, the three girls stuck close—an island of sophomores in an upperclassmen's domain.

Among those upperclassmen was Audrey Barton. Audrey was two years older than the girls, and well on her way to becoming the most successful senior in her class. She'd discovered Britt's room later than most, having waited until her junior year to fill her introductory art requirement. Once there, Audrey felt the force of Britt's energy, and found in art a natural ease. Now, in her final year at Narraguagus, Audrey had returned to take two more art classes. She'd also found herself gravitating to the art room, in its quiet moments, to work her way through college application and scholarship deadlines. Indeed, the room had become, for Audrey, a place from which to catapult her dreams. They were loftier dreams than most around these parts, and yet, in reaching for them, Audrey's feet stayed firmly planted on the ground.

Early in the fall term of Vivian's sophomore year, Britt assigned her Advanced Art students a project called *Tattoo You*, a self-exploration through biographical poetry and "body art" on the page. Britt watched Vivian compose her poem during class time—"Her face bright red, yanking on her hair with her left hand, sticking her pen in her mouth" with her right. When Vivian was done, one glance at the page from Britt was all it took. She knew this girl had talent, and a mind and heart so layered they might never be fully unearthed.

As the tattoo project progressed, Britt asked the students to read their poems to their classmates. They formed a circle around a cluster of tables in the front of the room. Vivian sat with her back to the windows, and when her turn came, the autumn sun stretched its weakened rays through speckled panes. She lifted her head with a shy gaze, blushed ever so slightly, and began to speak. At first, her voice was smooth and quiet. But as Vivian read, her tone and manner intensified, and her classmates sat taller. For, these were not the whispered secrets of a child, but the trumpets of a soul revealed.

Never disturb the moss, it takes seven years to heal,

And someday you may be healing and you will understand.

There may only be seven minutes.

Hurry

Savor

Do not disturb the moss, instead kiss the ground,

You are here to fall in love with who you are and everything there is,

Are you searching too?

It was a long poem, and unlike any other that would be heard that day, or even that year. And as Vivian drew to a close, her words took on the form of an exhortation.

I have one minute left of your time,

For it takes seven years for the moss to heal,

And seven minutes to tell you to hurry but savor, indulge, and inhale deeply. Love and you will smile, smile and you will love. Relax, find peace, learn, and grow. Do not wallow in despair, the darkest night brings the brightest sunrise.

You are not done, and you will never be done,

You must not be plucked from the earth only to wither into submission,

Do not let anyone confine your story to a book or a poem,

Because you are every word that has ever been spoken.

In the two years that followed the reading, Britt repeatedly urged Vivian to submit her poem to the Scholastic Art & Writing Awards. Each time, Vivian demurred. "She didn't think it was worthy," Britt recalled. In her senior year, Vivian finally acquiesced. The piece won a National Silver Medal.

It was also in her senior year that Vivian composed a memoir titled *Half-hearted Tragedy: A Recollection*. This, too, won a Scholastic award, a Regional Silver Key. But it was not the award that set the piece apart. It was the honesty of it. In this, a work her family did not read, Vivian marked her emergence from childhood in words that Britt would come to believe should be shared with every adolescent girl.

I was unaware of my own existence for seven years. The roots of self-consciousness had not yet taken their true form: unrelenting lip biting and hooded sweatshirts.

I can vaguely recall the first time I saw her, a stranger's face stapled to my underdeveloped body. I felt no change, no heavy weight placed upon my back, and saw no shift in the universe, but one silent pebble fell from the top of the pile, shattering the glassy unawareness of self. I came to recognize myself as an image instead of a thought, a discovery one does not ever come back from. In that moment, a child in wonder at her reflection, I did not understand the hatred of self. I did not understand enslave-

ment to a pane of glass, longing for its validation, existing only to gratify the gods of Beauty. I did not understand these things because I was only a child in awe of her own existence.

The pieces Vivian wrote were snippets of her life, sewn together, and laid bare. They were thick with abstraction, yet achingly revealing. Indeed, Vivian's adolescent life was as filled with paradox as the words she wrote. And the more Vivian worked to untangle the knots inside, the more her writings unmasked her pain.

Over the course of her Narraguagus years, Vivian would learn to navigate her hurt and ward away her demons. She would begin to recognize the better angels in her soul, and cast off the weight of family legacies beyond her control. She would also begin to see—and recoil from—the darker edges of her school culture. The way the alpha boys, often from lobster-fishing families, ruled the roost. The macho culture that seemed to give those alpha boys permission to mentally, sometimes physically, abuse their girlfriends. The arbitrary favoritism doled out by certain teachers to kids with surnames that mattered. The not so subtle way the girls' basketball team was placed on a pedestal and given a pass. The pain of those who came to school with nothing, and left with hastily hidden school pantry food. The silence behind the mask of differentness.

And even while Vivian remained loyal to the church to which she had been bound since birth, she would begin to doubt its teachings and its ways. It would turn, in her heart and mind, from a house of epiphany to a house of "fallacies," and begin to suffocate her soul. To free herself, she would find her way back to the blank page, the only place she felt safe enough to unleash her faltering faith. *In a single breath*, she would write, *I blamed myself, God, my mother, my father. I breathed more blame than air and in a moment I had become bitter as the marriage of toothpaste and orange juice.*

In the winter of her senior year, Vivian started dating Andy Carson, who lived in Houlton, 150 miles north of Harrington. Within a couple of months, the pair began to spend every weekend together, alternating travel between the two locations. Britt saw in Andy a contrast to the stream of local boys whom Vivian had previously allowed into her life. "I think Andy sees the beauty of Vivian's uniqueness," she observed, "and he's not going to suffocate her."

It was about that time, too, that Vivian sought to grapple with her health anxieties and invasive thoughts. She sat at her computer, late into the night, and googled the symptoms that had long been her most intimate partners. As she read, she realized that there was a label for what she'd experienced since childhood: OCD. The designation of a name on Vivian's inner turmoil empowered her. "The first person I told," she recalled, "was Frannie. I just knew that she would accept me, and she did. I also felt I really needed to tell Andy early in our relationship. When you first meet somebody, and you have something like that, it makes it so much worse not to open up. Frannie gave me the confidence to tell him." Andy listened, and embraced Vivian for who she was. For this, and for a multitude of other acts of openness and understanding, Andy was unlike anyone Vivian had known Downeast, "other than Frannie, of course." Vivian loved her parents with all her heart, but she never told them things that she told Andy and Frannie. "And," Vivian added slowly, "I probably never will."

Chapter 10

Upwind

When English teacher Ann-Marie Whalen saw "I hate faggits" scrawled in black ink across the poster, she knew her team would be in for a rough ride. *Bring it on*, she thought. *These kids can handle it*. The irony of the slur's misspelling wasn't lost on anyone, and it made the fifteen or so core members of the student-run civil rights team more determined to call it out. Ann-Marie's team coadviser, Pete Wilkins, suggested the students circle the graffiti, surround it with Christmas lights, and write beside it, "We're better than this." The team would make a lesson of the incident, as if to say, *This is why we're here*.

Vivian and Josie had been among the civil rights team leaders who'd crafted the original poster before it was defaced. Their effort was part of the newly formed group's plan to recognize the United Nations–sponsored International Tolerance Day. "The kids came up with an idea to have a booth decorated with dozens and dozens of pictures, of every different kind of human being," recalled Ann-Marie. "Students were encouraged to take a pledge of tolerance, then to go into the cafeteria and get their hand traced and colored in on a massive poster"—to form a giant rainbow.

The black-marker episode was just one instance of vandalism, ostensibly carried out by one student. But Ann-Marie and Pete saw it as a symbol of something they believed was being taught at home by too many families. They recognized it in the casual insults some kids flung across school corridors, the sneering looks at students who chose to dress and act differently from the others, and the derisive tone as they called the lunch area at which Latino students routinely gathered "the Mexican table." The worst student offenders, said Ann-Marie, "were a small group." But "they made their presence known."

If anyone had told a younger Ann-Marie she'd be coaching civil rights in northern Maine, she would have been surprised. Like Britt Frances, Ann-Marie had come "from away," and found her path Downeast later in life. She'd grown up in a suburban Massachusetts town, earned her bachelor's degree at the University of Massachusetts, then moved to Arizona to earn her master's and be near her retiree parents. While living in Arizona, Ann-Marie met her husband, Charles, and taught high school English. But after her parents died, she developed a longing to return to New England. Memories of honeymooning in Maine carried Ann-Marie and Charles back to the state, this time to settle. "We started looking at places to live in Maine," recalled Ann-Marie, "and we came across an ad for a house in Roque Bluff," a stunning oceanfront community twenty miles from Harrington. "I was on the phone with the realtor, and she asked what I did. When I said I was an English teacher, the realtor replied, 'Oh my gosh, my senior year English teacher just retired.'" Ann-Marie sent a letter of introduction to Narraguagus, and "two weeks later, I got a phone call from the principal, asking if I'd come up for an interview. Before I knew it, I'd ended up here."

By ending up here, Ann-Marie has helped reshape a generation of kids. Some call her controversial. At first glance, she hardly looks it. With her tailored clothes, silk scarves, and kitten-heel pumps, Ann-Marie is classically understated. But get her in a classroom, or talking about her goals for the kids she teaches, and the spark ignites. The roots of her passion came from her own journey with literature. "I am a reader," she said, "and words are how I make sense of . . . everything. I knew that if words could help turn a middle-class suburban Catholic girl into an advocate for people here who don't have all the advantages that I have had, maybe I could help young people discover the words that would pave their way to understanding more about the world."

For Ann-Marie, guiding students through Toni Morrison's *Beloved*, W. E. B. Du Bois's *The Souls of Black Folks*, and other works—and witnessing moments of realization and self-reflection as they read—was priceless. She pushed her students to think harder, to make connections between the books they read and the world around them. "She was," said Josie, "that teacher I rushed to see when I read something that gave me an idea. Or when I'd be in the library doing my online college courses, she was the one I sought out to discuss what I was learning. And she always brought more to it, and made me think more deeply." Likewise, for Vivian, Ann-Marie brought excitement to the realms of literature and human rights. She also showed "incredible compassion," said Vivian. "Some people think Mrs. Whalen is a bit off-putting," she added, "but they couldn't be more wrong about that. She's refined and cultured, and that can be intimidating. But she actually cares about your well-being."

Ann-Marie knew what some of the locals said about her manner and ideas; she also knew that for every raised eyebrow, there
were far more embraces of the lessons she put on center stage
in her classroom. "This is a conservative community, both politically and religiously, and I'm not either of those," said Ann-
Marie. In the classroom, "I don't discuss religion or politics,
because I firmly believe that's not my place. However, I am an
ardent believer in human rights, and because I teach literature,
things come up about people being treated badly by other people." To be sure, there were days when Ann-Marie wondered
how much weight her perspective carried. "Because I'm from
away," she would say, "I'm 'one of those people' with 'those
ideas,' and, to some, that means you can't trust much of anything
I say or do." And yet, it was clear that Ann-Marie drew respect,
even from those with divergent points of view. More than this,
Ann-Marie's lessons remained with many of her students long
after they'd left her classroom. They came to understand that, in
life, as in fishing, sometimes you needed to push against the tide.

For Ann-Marie's first decade or so at Narraguagus, teaching
progressed pretty much without incident. She knew her craft
well—and she guided her kids across literary bridges the likes of
which few Downeasters had seen. When kids acted out, as some
inevitably did, instead of being inordinately stern, she forged her
own path toward resolution. There were plenty of teachers who
urged her to keep a "firm hand," regardless of circumstances.
And indeed, Ann-Marie understood the need for structure and
rules. She was no stranger to the value of discipline and respect;
she herself had grown up with those lessons, and had carried
them forward to her own daughter. But Ann-Marie also understood that "the idea that, just because I'm the adult in the room,
I can demand respect without demonstrating it, is a completely

false place to start." When she saw kids acting out, she knew there was a reason. "You build a relationship, because you can't get very far with them if you don't. There's a lot of talk, a lot of jargon out there, but it all boils down to respect."

Ann-Marie recognized that she'd never gain her students' respect if she didn't demonstrate it. It took time and energy. But in the end, it worked. "You need to be able to say 'I'm sorry' when you screw up," she said. "It never ceases to amaze me that when I've apologized to a kid because I was frustrated, or I misinterpreted something—because you know, we're always misinterpreting something, by virtue of the different generations—and I go to a kid the next day and say, 'I'm sorry. I was rough on you yesterday, and I overreacted.' Then, so many times, they've looked at me like, 'Who are you? Are you some sort of Martian?' I've come to realize, that's not something many kids are accustomed to. And that is a problem within itself."

It was that simple idea of mutual respect that had sparked an unprecedented plan for Narraguagus High—the launch of a civil rights team. Picking up an initiative originally launched by Maine's attorney general years earlier, Ann-Marie and Pete embarked on the plan to challenge students' preconceptions. They wanted to push kids to consider what it might be like to look different, feel different, have different views from those who dominated their corner of the world.

The path that led to the team's formation, remembered Ann-Marie, was both exciting and troubling. It began with the principal, Lauren Donovan, who saw the possibility of doing more, and doing better, in the school—and the community—she loved. "Lauren knew," said Ann-Marie, "that if we were going to make progress, we needed to start with some serious introspection." Lauren brought in attorney and advocate Steve Wessler to help assess the path Narraguagus needed to travel to become safe and welcoming for all kids. Wessler had developed and led the Civil Rights Unit in the Maine Office of the Attorney General in the 1990s, and had since taken his show on the road.

Wessler began his work with Narraguagus by asking students to write down, anonymously, if—and how often—they'd been bullied or harassed. Lauren then called a mandatory staff training, which Wessler ran, at which he shared his findings. What the kids reported, recalled Ann-Marie, "was terrible. It ran a lot deeper than anyone had known or imagined." The list included bullying based on sexual orientation, and, added Pete, "girls getting harassed, getting slapped in the butt in the hallway, and being forced by boys to do things in the woods." And the number of times these incidents happened to each of the victims, recalled Ann-Marie, was "really high."

Lauren emerged from that meeting resolved to shake things up. Among the first steps was the launch of a schoolwide civil rights team. She tapped Pete first to organize it, and Ann-Marie jumped at the chance to join him. But the effort had to be student led, and Ann-Marie and Pete weren't sure who, if anyone, would show up to the thirty-minute weekly meetings they'd scheduled in the school library. They needn't have worried. Almost immediately, there was a steady flow of fifteen to twenty students. At first, they tended to be the kids who stood in the shadows, the ones who were so often overlooked. But they made themselves visible now, for they understood the weight of what they were about to create.

Then came more kids. In the team's early days, one who helped give the group "street cred," simply by being there, was Audrey Barton. She was the first athlete of note and the sole varsity girls' basketball team member to step up. Audrey was reticent by nature. She didn't speak often at the group's weekly meetings, but when she did, people listened. "Audrey is smart, beautiful, and very talented," recalled Ann-Marie. "She joined the CRT not because it looked good on her college applications or because she knew intimately what it was like to be marginalized. She has an intuitive empathy and decency that drives her." "She was," Pete added, "a natural leader. I really think she was there because she saw what was going on in the school and didn't think it was fair, and she used her star power to say, 'You can't do this.'"

Two other students whom Ann-Marie and Pete credited with landing the team on the Narraguagus map were Vivian and Josie. They were unflinching, and they jumped headlong into the team's most controversial forays. In 2015, the nascent group sponsored an LGBTQ awareness day. Team members distributed posters to the homerooms, Ann-Marie recalled, "asking teachers and students to wear shirts that represented the colors of the rainbow as a sign of support for all LGBTQ people." Teachers were asked to wear one color and each grade was assigned another color, and on the appointed day, "everyone who participated was to gather in the gym for a group rainbow photo." Some teachers refused to take a poster. Some students ripped the posters from the walls. Phone calls to Lauren "started ringing off the hook" and "social media exploded."

Irate parents demanded action. "They were saying, 'Who do they think they are? How dare they?'" Ann-Marie remembered. "Then, some of the teachers went to Lauren, and said, 'How can you allow this? I'm not going to participate.'" They were, recalled Ann-Marie, a small but vocal group, who opposed any actions that "drew attention" to "those kids." In response, the team put up new posters, clarifying that the event was voluntary. It was too late. Feeling the heat, the district superintendent nudged Lauren to call it off. Lauren didn't agree that calling off the event would make things better; indeed, she thought it might make things worse. "She had our back, and she believed in what we were doing. She ran interference, and didn't even tell us," recalled Ann-Marie. "It was incredibly brave of her."

The event went off as planned, resulting, said Ann-Marie, in "a frenzy of negativity." At the same time, there were "dozens of emails and texts from members of the community and graduates in support of what the team was doing." The back-and-forth on social media was so charged that Lauren suspended the use of classroom laptops. Some parents took their kids out of school for the day. For several days after the event, recalled Ann-Marie, the turmoil continued. "Lauren was going to lose her job. Pete and I were going to lose our jobs. So, we finally decided that if we were going to continue with a longer-term student-led rights agenda, we needed to go to the school board to talk things out."

In autumn of the next school year, as the civil rights team began to plan for a second LGBTQ awareness day, it also prepared to make its case to the school board and superintendent. Vivian wrote and submitted a letter discussing the team's goals and highlighting its action plan. "We realize," she wrote, "there was heavy controversy regarding last year's LGBTQ event. Understanding the confusion, and wishing to avoid similar miscommunication, we are openly informing you . . . of our intentions for this event. The purpose of this event is to educate students about the impact of a hostile and unsupportive school and community climate as well as the benefits to the entire community of tolerance and acceptance. . . . Positive contributions to a respectful learning environment include speaking up when hearing negative comments and acting in a respectful manner toward everyone, regardless of appearance, sexual orientation, gender identity, race, or religion."

Ann-Marie would never forget the scene at the meeting as school board members took up the debate. "One said, 'God knows them people ain't right' as he misquoted Scripture," she recalled. "Another questioned our patriotism, erroneously claiming that we were trying to get rid of the Pledge of Allegiance." One asked, 'Is this really something we need to be introducing to kids?' and argued, 'We don't have those kids here. We don't have people like that in our community.'" But then, too, there were others. There were members and parents and community on-lookers "who took on the voice of reason," or sat, uncomfort-ably, in growing disbelief at the unfolding drama. After about an hour and a half, "one board member, who had been silent up to that point, asked to speak, and she basically said this: 'Thirty-six years ago, I was hauled into the Narraguagus principal's office and told I could no longer attend school because I was pregnant. I was humiliated, I was devastated, and I was later shunned by the community. I was made to feel as if I was dirty and bad. And I don't know that I understand about all this stuff. I don't even know what all those letters mean. But I know that if kids are made to feel that there's something wrong with them, that's wrong. And if we can help one kid not feel the way I felt, then this is the right thing to do.'" When the board member stopped, recalled Ann-Marie, the room went silent. Then, after a while, someone said, "I think we better wrap this up." And they were done.

Ann-Marie saw in that meeting reasons to celebrate girls like Vivian and Josie, and to find hope in their generation's willing-ness to push for change. They're "extraordinary young women," she observed. "They would be extraordinary in any community, under any circumstances. What they have in common is they both come from very culturally, religiously conservative families, they're both leaders, they're both extremely intelligent, and they're both artists." Their commitment to the civil rights team, in the context of their family background, "took courage. And I believe that both of them would say that through their experiences, they also evolved tremendously as human beings."

Ann-Marie knew that she and some in this community would never march in lockstep. And yet she would not choose to live anywhere else, to be a part of anything other than the education and growth of these, the children of Downeast. She knew that, for many of them, the road was not easy. "I especially see it with the kids who say, 'I just have to get away from here for a while.' But then," added Ann-Marie, "many of them are the same kids who cherish their community. It's very much a 'you can't go home again' kind of thing, like that umbilical cord that you can't quite cut, although, sometimes, you'll stretch it as far as you can."

Through her own journey, Ann-Marie came to understand "that these young people will be the lifeline for Downeast Maine." Their love for their families and hometowns is unconditional, but, as Ann-Marie observed, this new generation does not abide "intolerance or clannish isolation." She sees the proof of this in girls like Audrey, Vivian, and Josie. "While much of the country sees a rural backwater lacking in sophistication and urbane sensibilities," said Ann-Marie, "these girls belie that characterization. They see beauty in this place and in the people they love; they've embraced hope, and have chosen their paths with insight and courage."

Chapter 11

Digging for Gold

It was winter again Downeast. Most of the local lobster boats sat idle. Their owners had tucked away the notebooks on which they'd tallied their earnings, and piled their traps high and deep in their dooryards. This time of year, the weather was boss, so if you'd had a decent run, there was no sense fighting it. A handful of fishermen would continue to haul straight through to spring, some out of necessity, others because it had always been done that way. Down at Holt's Wharf, there was enough profit from summer and fall to allow the family to kick back through the harshest months, but Mckenna's dad and brother Matthew pressed on just the same. There was no shame in keeping the work going, and no shortage of lobsters to be found, if you set your traps out far enough in warmer water. For her part, Mckenna had stopped fishing by Thanksgiving. The *River Rodent* was an inshore boat, too small to follow the lobsters as they migrated out to sea. And as much as Mckenna hoped to haul off the coast someday, she could do without the predawn skirmishes with icy waters to get to where the traps lay waiting.

On land or sea, winters here are unforgiving. The winds taunt their trespassers, the cold cuts like steel, and the sun withdraws by half past three. If you're looking for good indoor diversions, you'll have to plan ahead. The nearest movie theater is more than an hour away. The closest bowling lanes sit forty minutes west of Narraguagus High. A few months back, the sole pizza place in Harrington closed down. It had pretty good takeout, but the owner couldn't make the numbers work.

Given the options, it was little wonder that Narraguagus's girls' basketball was the go-to choice for cold-weather entertainment. This year, as the first game approached, Mckenna nearly jumped with anticipation. She was no stranger to varsity ball; she'd been a part of it since she'd entered Narraguagus as a freshman. But in this, her senior year, Mckenna had risen to the rank of co-captain. And the word around town was that this particular squad had that Gold Ball glow—that this collection of Lady Knights, perhaps more than any other since that memorable championship-winning day in 2016, had an honest-to-goodness shot at the title.

At the season's first tip-off, locals filed into the high school's high-gloss gym. It hadn't been long since the community had anted up with higher property taxes for a full gym makeover. Folks would remark that the new facility was every bit as good as the ones those fancy schools paraded in southern Maine. Narraguagus had even gone the extra mile and added livestreaming, giving those lucky enough to have reliable internet the option of tuning in from home. And while the boys' varsity team regularly drew healthy crowds, it was the girls' team, still glowing from the magic of its 2016 victory, that filled the bleachers.

This year, enthusiasm mingled with apprehension. In August, two and a half years after leading the girls' team to its Gold Ball victory, Olivia Marshall had announced her resignation as varsity coach. By all accounts, she'd stepped down on the news of her father-in-law's cancer diagnosis. But Olivia had also become frustrated by the misplaced priorities of some parents, the way their overzealousness had begun to infiltrate the girls.

As word spread that the heralded coach had resigned, locals began to talk. Everyone knew that in the two seasons that had followed the state championship win, things had changed. People whispered about it: the pressure some parents had increasingly placed on their girls; the sniping about who was being played and when; the game-time scowls and mouthing off, obvious from across the court to Olivia and the girls. "I call it parent goggles," Olivia would say. "They put 'em on, and all they see is their kid. Instead of stepping back and allowing their daughter to work for a spot on her own, they're stepping in and trying to bully."

Olivia had cringed as belligerence from the stands had begun to spill over to the players' bench. In the seasons that followed the 2016 victory, the teams had continued to show promise, but the chemistry that had propelled the Lady Knights to the top had disappeared. "To be sure," said Olivia, "we'd had some rough times in 2016. Girls are going to bicker, and they have their moods. But in the end, they all had a common goal. They knew they could win. They knew they had to respect each other, that they each had their own job. And if they did their job, they were gonna succeed."

The drop-off from the Lady Knights' Gold Ball heights became clear during the pressure-cooker playoffs of 2018. That season, the team went 17-2, and made it to the tournament's quarterfinal round. As the tournament's number three seed, it was favored over its longtime rival, the eleventh-seeded Calais Blue

Devils. But Calais, which had won the Gold Ball seven times since girls' teams had started playing in the state tournament in 1975, was always a worry for Narraguagus. And when the Lady Knights took to the court to battle Calais, they couldn't find the magic. The upset stung Olivia and the girls, and it knocked the wind out of the hopeful hometown crowd. The caravan ride home was long and somber. It was early February, and much of the bitter Downeast winter still lay ahead.

Mckenna had been a junior starter on that team. Now, at the launch of her first season without Olivia at the helm, she was as anxious as she was excited. Looking back, Mckenna shook her head at the tensions that had fueled Olivia's resignation. "That's what it all came down to," said Mckenna, "parents thinking their kid should be the star. And it ripped our team apart." Whenever Olivia tried to get the girls to play as a team, "she'd get hit by parents saying, 'I've put all this time and money into my kid.' It was a lose-lose situation."

For her part, Olivia knew she'd miss being on that Narraguagus basketball court as much as Mckenna would miss having her there. She'd spent countless hours on it—starting with her own high school playing career in the 1990s. When she married Brady and began to fish and start a family, she hoped that someday she might return to coach at Narraguagus. Indeed, it was not long after Olivia finished high school that she started coaching basketball at a nearby elementary school. She continued to coach—moving to her Narraguagus role in 2015—even when time was short and money was tight in the Marshall household.

There was no doubt that Olivia's days, blessed as they were, were long. She was out the door by 5:00 a.m., hauling traps until midafternoon, scrambling home to be there for her boys, or heading straight to the gym for practice. On away-game days, Olivia and the girls would return to the Narraguagus parking lot hours after the sun had set. The miles between them and their competitors seemed endless, with barely a traffic light in sight. Still, Olivia considered herself lucky to be able to fill her days with the three things she loved most: family, fishing, and basketball.

Through it all, Olivia maintained an aura of lightness that belied the grind of her days. She'd long ago learned that she'd only reap as much as she poured into her labors, "that no one else was going to do it for you." Outsiders and locals alike would marvel at the way she had broken barriers with her fishing career. But Olivia insisted there was nothing special about it. She was "a fourth-generation lobsterman" who was simply doing what she loved. She looked at Mckenna, and the growing number of girls who'd chosen to make a living through lobstering, and she saw doors flying open for them. The industry had grown "so much bigger" than when she and Brady had gotten into it, twenty-five years earlier. "There's a lot more money," Olivia would remark, "and a lot more opportunity to jump on a boat." In the Marshalls' early days, "there were maybe seven boats" moored at Harrington's Town Landing. Today, the landing boasted more than twenty-five "very expensive" vessels— each valued at $450,000 or more.

Olivia had coached many of the girls who'd opted to fish, and she'd felt a rush of pride every time one of them told her, "After watching you, I know I can do it." You could still count on one hand the number of local female captains. But more and more girls, and women, were taking on the role of sternman, the captain's lynchpin who baits, empties, and drops the traps off the side of the boat, and bands the lobsters that are big enough to keep. Indeed, in recent years, Olivia had seen some male captains go out of their way to hire women. "They know," she said, "that women are more reliable. If they tell you they're going to be there at a certain time, they'll be there. They're not going to ditch you. They want to do the work, and they don't mind getting their hands dirty. They can step back and realize, 'I'm pretty lucky to have this chance.'"

Lucky indeed. That's exactly how Olivia felt whenever she looked back on how far she and Brady had come. Nearly a quarter century had passed since the couple had bought their first boat, the *Ledge Marker*, from Brady's uncle for nine thousand dollars. They'd borrowed off credit cards to pay what they owed in increments. Now, Olivia and Brady owned four "dream boats," whose combined value exceeded a million dollars. Olivia had named the newest of these the *Gold Digger*, in honor of the championship-winning Narraguagus team. The *Gold Digger* was all Olivia—sleek and sturdy, its lettering etched boldly in black and gold, its hull shining atop glassy waters. Olivia couldn't imagine a better expression of who she was—or a more fitting tribute to her odds-beating girls.

Now, as winter idled, the *Gold Digger* stood grounded. At Christmastime, the Marshalls decked it with three thousand lights—adorning the vessel's every possible plank and stretch. They raised a glass of gratitude, and bade the *Gold Digger* good night, so that it might begin its season of well-earned rest. Come spring, it would find its way back to the water, where it belonged. So, too, it was for Olivia. As she bided her time until she could fish again, she settled in with Brady to watch the Lady Knights' opener from the Marshalls' specially designated Narraguagus seats—and hoped that her good fortune might find its way to the team she used to coach.

Christmas came and went. The land turned brittle and the branches moaned under the weight of their crystalline garb. Chimneys blew white billows from the homes of those fortunate enough to claim a fireplace. Trailers hummed softly as space heaters inside worked overtime.

Still, the Downeast shoreline did not sleep. Persistent fishermen pressed their boats outward, following lobsters in their hunt for warmer seabeds. Across wide flats, clam diggers waited for the tide to ebb, then hastily plucked their payloads from the rocky sands. There was no time to waste before the waters rose again.

At days' end, these laborers washed the silt from their bodies, piled their children into icy trucks, and wound their way to Narraguagus High to cheer for their beloved Lady Knights.

This year, the girls had done them proud. Indeed, after a season-opening loss to perennial powerhouse Calais, the Lady Knights had managed to emerge undefeated the rest of the way. They'd beaten their remaining opponents handily, sometimes winning by 40 points or more. In the regular season's final matchup, the squad faced Calais again. This time, Narraguagus prevailed. With the tournament just around the corner, the girls and their fans could taste the possibility of a Gold Ball championship redux.

On Valentine's Day, Mckenna turned eighteen, and she was exuberant. Two days earlier, she and her teammates had trounced the Searsport Vikings in the first round of tournament play. As Mckenna prepared for the quarterfinal round in Bangor, she found herself thinking a lot about the team's unlikely 2016 win. She'd not only been the youngest Lady Knight to play in that championship basketball game, but at five feet two, she had been, without a doubt, the shortest. She'd also been nervous as hell. Hours before the game she'd thrown up twice. And every warm-up cheer from the stands had reminded her just how much winning the Gold Ball would mean to the hometown crowd. After the team's heart-stopping victory, Mckenna had looked on with pride as Audrey Barton and her fellow co-captains climbed onto a ladder, removed the netting from the center court, and distributed pieces of it to their teammates as keepsakes. Three years later, Mckenna's twisted fragment of twine still hung from her bookbag. Over the years, Mckenna had often found herself reaching absentmindedly for that particular shred of nostalgia. Its edges had frayed, and its knots had been polished flat. Now, Mckenna imagined the moment that she might climb up, just as Audrey had, and cut away a new memento for the Lady Knights.

The quarterfinal against Penobscot Valley was just five days away. Mckenna and her teammates had left school early for a scrimmage against Deer Isle-Stonington High School, an hour-and-a-half bus ride away. As the scrimmage wound down, Mckenna began to look forward to her evening birthday plans. Then, abruptly, Mckenna stopped. She'd misstepped somehow, and now, she let out a faint groan as her ankle crumpled beneath her. Damn, she thought, this can't be good.

When the doctors at Ellsworth's Northern Light Maine Coast Hospital told Mckenna to stay off her leg for six weeks, she swore she heard four days. Meanwhile, Phoebe put out an urgent Facebook call for home remedies. Advice poured in from every corner of Downeast Washington County. Wraps, stretches, soaks, and essential oils—for the seventy-two hours that followed,

Mckenna and Phoebe worked them all. By game day, Mckenna was braced up and ready to play.

Mckenna saw court time during most of the quarterfinal contest. The pain in her leg ran through to her fingertips, but she wasn't about to show it. For much of the game, Narraguagus trailed by double digits. Grim faces dotted the Lady Knights' section of the stands. Then, Narraguagus staged a late-game comeback to shrink Penobscot Valley's lead to six. With seconds left on the clock, Mckenna landed a three-pointer, and suddenly Narraguagus had an outside chance at victory. The hometown crowd rose with a collective roar, then held its breath. The girls held theirs too, even as they held out hope—for themselves; for their new coach, who'd stepped up from his role as Olivia's assistant and had proven himself to be skilled and kind and motivating; for their supporters; and for Olivia, who'd cheered them on every step of the way. But in the end, it was not meant to be.

No matter, Mckenna consoled herself, as she packed up her gear and pulled the brace from her aching leg. In time, the ground would thaw, and the lobsters would find their way back inshore. And the pattern of Downeast life would begin anew.

Part Three

Across the Bridge

Chapter 12

Home

Every so often, Audrey Barton wondered if she'd made the right choice in leaving Bates. She knew that switching to University of Maine at Orono after her freshman year made sense, but at the moment, she wasn't feeling particularly challenged. Now in her junior year, she had racked up so many academic credits that she was nearly done with her requirements. She'd briefly considered the possibility of graduating early, but the few classes she needed weren't offered in the right sequence. So Audrey doubled down on her UMO commitments and made the most of her extra time. She worked in the psych lab, ran for officers' roles in two speech and language associations, and carried on with her volunteer work for Best Buddies.

She also continued to plan for the future. If she wanted to practice as a licensed speech pathologist, she'd have to pursue a two-year master's degree. On that front, Audrey had little cause for concern; she'd have no trouble getting into a graduate program. She'd been a dean's list regular, and had earned induction into an international honor society, reserved for the top 15 percent of students in colleges and universities. Audrey hadn't done badly at Bates either, where, as a premed student, she'd practically earned straight As. No one questioned her smarts, or her commitment to academics. But just as she had when she'd graduated Narraguagus, she once again felt the tug of remaining close to home. She knew she could apply to graduate schools beyond Maine's borders—with a decent shot at getting into a highly competitive program. But her heart still lay Downeast.

The fact was, that tug had been the reason for Audrey's transfer to UMO two years earlier. To some, her move was surprising. By leaving Bates and intercollegiate basketball behind, Audrey had closed a door that she'd worked hard to open in high school—and had walked away from a prize that few from her hometown could ever dream of grasping.

Yet, the few times Audrey had found herself wondering if she'd made the right decision, it didn't take more than a good look at all she had Downeast—and all that she could build within it—to remind her that her choice was spot on.

Suzanne was certain too. She knew that Audrey hoped for a career with meaning, something that might help ease the road for others around her. She and Mike had raised Audrey to lead with a strong heart. They felt fortunate that their three surviving children also had strong minds, and the sensibility to put them to good use.

Suzanne also knew that there was no shortage of need Downeast for qualified speech and language practitioners. With the right credentials, Audrey could earn good money, and for girls Downeast, that mattered. "I always told my kids, and especially my girls," she said, "'I don't care what you do but I want you to always be able to take care of yourself. I don't want you to ever have to depend on a husband—or anybody else.'" Suzanne had seen "so many people get stuck in a relationship, and stay in it." They'd justify their decision by saying, "Well, you know I need to eat. My kids need to eat." But Suzanne told her own kids, again and again, "You never need to get stuck. I want them to be independent enough that if they're in a relationship, wherever it ends up, they have choices. I want them to be their own person."

Suzanne never stopped urging Audrey to consider her options carefully, even as Audrey rose to the top of her Narraguagus class and proved herself skilled in nearly every pursuit. Indeed, Suzanne had cautioned her, "Don't go get an education you can't use if you don't want to move away from here." But the Bates offer was alluring, and the chance to play basketball there was thrilling. It wasn't the kind of opportunity a girl from Downeast, or for that matter, from pretty much anywhere, turned down lightly.

The question was, what to study? And how to turn her academic pursuits into a career that would allow her to return Downeast and make a living? Only when Audrey stood at the crossroads of her Bates education did the answer come to her. She started job shadowing, working with kids who struggled with speech and language—and she fell in love with the work. It was then, Suzanne recalled, that the Bartons began to realize that "she'd have to be done at Bates—because it's strictly a liberal arts school."

Audrey had explored how she might stay at Bates and get the credentials she'd need to work in speech and language pathology. But the path forward wasn't obvious. What's more, the list of reasons to move northward was long. There was Audrey's boyfriend, Jack, for starters. Audrey had begun dating Jack in her sophomore year at Narraguagus. More than five years later, the pair was not officially engaged, but they'd long been making plans to marry soon after Audrey graduated college. Jack had grown up in a tight-knit family in the Bangor area, just down the road from UMO. Now, he worked Downeast, at a bank branch in Machias. When Audrey first considered her Bates option, she'd tried not to let its distance from Jack, and from her own family, influence her. But over time, the miles between them, and the unfamiliarity of the Bates environment, had crept into Audrey's consciousness and pressed their weight upon her. True, she'd made some friends on campus, and she'd found some connections that had helped ease her transition. As part of a "first-generation" program, she'd joined thirty or so other students whose parents hadn't gone to college for a week's worth of campus events before the start of her freshman year. That helped, as did the time she spent with her basketball teammates. Still, Audrey couldn't quite find her footing. In those early Bates months, she'd maintained strong ties to her family, high school friends, and community—and had continued to center much of her life around them. "When you're in a small community you know everybody," she'd reflect. "Even when you go to outer towns, like Machias, you still probably know most people. Then, you go to Bates, and all of a sudden you don't know anyone. There were students from so many different places. And even though that was pretty cool, because you get to meet a lot of new people, it was also unfamiliar."

In the weeks leading up to her transfer, Audrey emailed back and forth with the faculty member who would ultimately become her adviser at UMO's Communications and Sciences Disorders department. "She basically said, 'You should stay at Bates,'" said Audrey. "That the education there was very valuable. And she gave me the contact information of a person who used to be her graduate assistant who was able to graduate from Bates" by taking a leave to complete the specialized classes she'd needed at UMO. "I talked to her," said Audrey, "and it just didn't change my mind." What's more, unlike Bates, UMO was willing to accept the online college credits Audrey had earned while at Narraguagus High. In the end, Audrey reflected, "I could have gotten a degree at Bates, but I wouldn't have used it. I still would've had to get a year's worth of prerequisites somewhere else just to apply to graduate school."

So it was that Audrey found her way to UMO, and through it, discovered a place that would carry her forward with comfort and familiarity. The life that Audrey, Jack, and her family had collectively chosen to pursue was just down the road. And everything she needed to build that life was at her doorstep.

The summer between Audrey's junior and senior years of college was fast approaching. Once again, Audrey planned to rev up the *No Interest* and haul lobsters. It was the best way for her to earn, and continue to save, some money. She knew she wouldn't make much through whatever job she might land after graduation, most likely in speech and language pathology—at least not until she'd earned her master's. Even after Audrey graduated, as long as she could make the schedule work, she'd likely continue to summer fish. And although she didn't enjoy it, she was grateful it would always be there for her.

In March, Jack had begun taking online courses toward a bachelor's degree in Fire Science. He'd long hoped to break away from his customer service job at the bank; for a while, he'd considered enlisting in the military. Now, he'd set his sights on joining the ranks of firefighters in Bangor or Ellsworth, or perhaps in one of the Acadia-centered towns on Mount Desert Island. The small towns that dotted Downeast Washington County didn't offer a viable option; their fire departments were all volunteer. If Audrey and Jack's plan panned out, the couple would look to settle a few miles down the road from Milbridge "in a town as far Downeast as we can go, so that we can still be close to both my parents and his," while allowing Jack a reasonable commute.

In the meantime, Audrey looked forward to a summer at home on the Back Bay Road. She'd had her license long enough, and had put in enough hours over the years, to fish as many as seven hundred traps. But she'd be content to haul two to three hundred, with her dad as sternman. She also hoped to fit in some job shadowing with kids who were getting speech and language services, either in Machias or at Narraguagus High. Plus, she could carve out some time to study for the GRE exam, which she planned to take in August.

Audrey figured that hauling a couple of times a week would give her what she needed, moneywise. She could opt for the 3:00 or 4:00 a.m. shift, leaving the house in darkness, as her dad and brothers routinely did to fish. Or she could wait for her father to return from his morning haul, so that the pair might squeeze hers in before the sun went down. Either way, she'd keep her summer fishing routine going, just as she had since she'd first apprenticed more than a decade earlier. As her dad had constantly reminded her when she was younger, there wasn't a summer job around where she could make better money. He'd tell her, "You can go work at the grocery store if you want to, but you've got to realize you have to put in eight hours a day, and you're not gonna make much money." It didn't take long for Audrey to do the math and know he was right. As Suzanne would say,

"There's nothing like money to motivate Audrey to work on the lobster boat." Suzanne would add with a smile, "If she gets a job as a school speech language pathologist, and somehow she falls in love with fishing and can't get it out of her blood," Audrey could fish her summers away for years to come.

The arc of Audrey's life was not unlike that of other top-achieving girls from Narraguagus—and from similar schools across rural America. From the point of view of many urban and suburban young people, Audrey's choices may have seemed out of step. But for Audrey, they were transcendently logical and rational. They would have the extra benefit, too, of helping energize and perpetuate towns like Milbridge, Harrington, and Cherryfield. If all went according to plan, between Audrey's speech and language work and Jack's firefighting, the couple would provide much-needed services to the Downeast community. They'd contribute to the area in more personal ways too: by having kids and sending them to the local schools; by being civically engaged; and by helping care for their parents and other extended family members as they age. In the broadest terms, Audrey's path defines "local success." Choices like hers are as valuable as gold to rural communities like those Downeast. They kindle optimism for the future.

Chapter 13

Adrift

On an unremarkably frigid morning, the Narraguagus students began to assemble in the school's front hall, much as they always did. Then *BAM*—and silence, and everyone turned to stare. Two boys emerged, pushing and grabbing. Punches flew, and the growing crowd pulled back. The fight was on.

The morning show ended as quickly as it began, as three teachers scrambled to pull the pair apart. One of the boys wiped blood from his face. The other stood frozen, fists still clenched, eyes defiant. Lauren Donovan ushered both boys into her office and shut the door, while the morning duty staff shepherded the rest of the kids along. It was just another day at Narraguagus High.

Moments later, the hallways rippled with the *click, click, click* of closing classroom doors, and Willow plopped contentedly in a corner of the empty cafeteria. She tugged at Eeyore's leash, and he tugged back playfully, nearly knocking her flat. She offered him a treat, and smoothed his close-cropped fur. Eeyore was Willow's newest addition, a rollicking eight-month-old mix of Saint Bernard and bullmastiff. She called him her baby, and showered him with love.

Willow had graduated and was nearing the end of her first semester at University of Maine at Machias. She had started the term revved up to work toward her business degree. Then she'd begun to drift. She had returned to Narraguagus, as she was doing this day, nearly a dozen times, to visit Frannie or hang out with friends who hadn't yet graduated. Those friends still called Willow "Mom," the name they'd bestowed on her years earlier as a tribute to her nurturing soul. She'd decided to take most of her freshman classes online, and she'd recently shelved her long-term plan to open a photography studio. Throughout Willow's senior year at Narraguagus, the camera had been a fixture around her neck. Now she took pictures only occasionally, as a favor to friends who needed a headshot done. She'd also begun to question the value of college. She was willing to stick it out at UMM for spring semester, but beyond that, she wasn't sure the journey was worth the time.

Shortly before Willow's Narraguagus graduation, she'd gotten engaged to her boyfriend, Lee. The pair had met when she was sixteen, while Willow was living with Grandma Ann. But even though Willow thought of Ann as "the most amazing person" in her life, the one who had sheltered and cared for her time and time again as a child, she'd bristled under her grandmother's watchful eye as a teenager. Willow hadn't lived with Ann since puberty, and Ann wasn't used to her "wanting to go and hang out with boys and be with friends, or even play sports." She certainly didn't approve of Willow having a boyfriend. She would tell Willow, *Just come home, eat, sleep, do your homework, and then go back to school*. But Willow had started something with her life that she "didn't want to quit." And so she left, and in so doing, temporarily severed her relationship with her maternal grandmother.

With nowhere else to go, Willow had moved back, briefly, with her mom, stepdad, and two brothers in Steuben. But the house wasn't big enough for all of them. So Willow had ended up spending most of that summer at Lee's parents' house, while her mom and stepdad prepared to make room for her to return to them in the fall. They bought a trailer for her to live in and began to set it up next to their home. Willow was hopeful that the arrangement would work. She hadn't lived with her mom in many years, and she longed to be able to settle there, beside her. But when the time came, Willow balked. Her first night in the trailer, she started "having an anxiety attack." In part, she missed the life she'd begun to build at Lee's house, the steady routine of it, and his parents' warm embrace of her. In part, she feared she'd have trouble being around her stepdad's family, who lived next door. They reminded Willow of her own family—the way, as in her own childhood, she was "not allowed to show emotions." The way "you have to say yes, you can't say anything, and you can't question anything." The next day, Willow told her mom she wasn't comfortable staying there—and broke the news that Lee's parents had asked her to return and live with them full time. Lily turned to Willow and said, *You've always made the right decision. You're the reason you've gotten this far.* And she let her go.

Now, two years later, that time felt like a distant memory to Willow. She'd long been living with Lee and his parents, she'd reconciled with Grandma Ann, and things with her mom and stepdad were running smoothly. It was around this time, too, that Willow had found herself in a new, and better, chapter with her dad. The road to reconciliation had been slow. It had begun in the winter of Willow's senior year at Narraguagus, when a text from William flashed across Willow's screen. *I'm clean*, she'd remembered him saying. *I've been clean for three months. Tell me what I can do to help you, because I haven't been the father I was supposed to be.* And so Willow moved toward her father, carefully, and with trepidation. But also, with hope. Willow knew that there would always be an unspoken barrier between them, that they would "never have the father-daughter relationship a lot of people have." But perhaps, she thought, they might find peace within the space they shared.

Willow and William's path forward rested, in part, on the pair's common goal of starting a business of their own. As Willow began to navigate her first months at UMM, William latched on to his latest moneymaking fantasy: a marijuana dispensary in nearby Jonesport. The idea was sparked by Maine voters' razor-thin approval of a recreational legalization ballot measure in 2016. William and other hopeful pot retailers were intrigued by the possibility that they might be allowed to open their doors by the coming spring. But with their fate resting in the hands of state regulators, it was anyone's guess when the green light might come. Willow figured her dad had as good a chance as anyone at snagging a license. He certainly had plenty of experience with the product; he'd been growing and smoking it for decades. But, said Willow, "he knows nothing about how to run a business." That's where she came in.

Willow was drawn to the idea, and she'd begun to map out a business plan in her head. She and Lee were also figuring on the opportunity to run the modest bait business his grandparents owned. "When Lee's grandparents pass," said Willow, "they're planning to leave the business" to him. The transfer was likely years away, but Willow didn't want to be caught unprepared. She started learning everything she could about the industry. Over the years, she'd picked up a fair bit working at the wharf—and watching the Westfords run a thriving ice-fishing bait shop from the oversized garage on their property. Those glimpses helped, but they didn't match the knowledge that came with growing up in a fishing family. Willow hadn't been schooled at the dinner table on the finer points of herring and hauls, or heard her parents gripe about "those damn regulators" and worry about the future of the industry, the way Audrey and Mckenna had. Indeed, the knowledge Willow sought wasn't the kind you'd find in a textbook or on a how-to video. It was passed down and cultivated through work and family—and faith that a higher power would guide its bearers toward prosperity.

Willow yearned to someday give her children those lessons and memories, to create a world for them Downeast whose foundation rested on all that was good within it. She also held on to hope that her own parents might extend to her the nurturing she'd known so little of as a child. She found it, in part, through her mom, who'd recently taken the unlikely step of enrolling at UMM to pursue a college degree. Even though Willow hadn't always been with her mom—indeed, she'd spent much of her young life living apart from Lily—she'd always been attached to her. Now, Willow had the chance to reconnect on a different footing. And there was no question in Willow's mind that Lily's presence was the best part of her freshman UMM experience.

Lily had spent most of her adult life working as a nurse's aide with families and at the local nursing home. But along the way, she'd hurt her back on the job. When she could no longer do the heavy lifting the work routinely required, she'd faced the choice of quitting or going back to school for skills that might give her better options. So Lily gathered her resolve, and decided to pursue a bachelor's in nursing. With it, she'd have a good shot at a decent-paying, less physically demanding hospital job in Bangor or Ellsworth. Lily's decision fit perfectly with Willow's early memories of her mom. As kids, Willow and her brothers had often heard Lily say how much she'd liked being in school, how she wished she'd been able to continue after graduating from Narraguagus. Each time Willow had listened to her mom speak wistfully about what she'd lost by cutting her education short, she'd blamed herself. "She didn't get to go to college because of me," Willow would say, "because she got pregnant with me."

Now, in her late thirties, with her daughter once again by her side, Lily had made it to her second year of nursing coursework. Willow could see the pride in Lily's eyes each time she showed her daughter the UMM ropes—guiding her toward the best teachers; helping her think through the sequence of courses she'd need to complete; offering her the moral support she'd craved so often in her earlier years, when their lives had been caught in the darkness between dusk and dawn.

Willow practically beamed as she considered the time she'd spent with Lily since starting college. Even now, the pair was making plans to take a math class together in the spring, "fighting through the pain," arm in arm. Indeed, math was the only spring-semester course that Willow wouldn't be taking online. When she'd thought about it, she'd said, "I'd much prefer taking math with my mom than with anyone else." Looking ahead, Willow longed for her college experiences with Lily to carry on. But she also knew that they might soon end. UMM had announced it was phasing out Lily's program, which had, until then, let nurses with only a hospital diploma or associate's degree pursue a Bachelor of Science in Nursing. Come September, Lily would have to go elsewhere if she wanted to finish her degree.

Macro trends played a part in both the opening and closing of Lily's opportunity at UMM. Rural America is home to nearly one-fourth of our nation's adult women—who, as a group, have lower levels of educational attainment and higher levels of poverty than urban women. They also have significantly fewer college graduates, more household incomes below the poverty level, poorer overall health outcomes, and less access to health-care services than urban women—including limited access to obstetrics and prenatal care. Private health insurance is often considered a luxury; a higher percentage of rural women rely on Medicaid and Medicare than their urban counterparts. Moreover, rural women have had the highest rates of "delayed care or no medical care" in the nation due to cost.

As a response to these challenges, and in the face of warnings by hospitals and nursing associations of an impending statewide—and national—nurse shortage (a prominent 2017 study asserted that Maine would face a gap of 3,200 nurses by 2025), leaders at the UMaine system crafted a five-year plan to double nursing enrollments. They stepped up outreach and recruitment efforts. To reach more rural students, they added one thousand additional online nursing studies slots. And in 2018, Maine's voters approved a $49 million bond issue, matched by $49 million in public and private funds, for workforce initiatives, including the expansion of nursing programs, across UMaine's campuses.

Lily, and others like her seeking the opportunity to earn a better living and be among those who would make a difference for their communities, became part of a wave of nursing

enrollments across Maine. Within three years, the state's mul-
tipronged strategy had yielded results. Today, Maine is among
forty-three states that expect a surplus of nurses by 2030.

In Willow's final English class of the semester, the professor
had asked her students to consider the best and worst aspects of
their first months at UMM. One of the questions she'd pressed
them to answer was, *Why are you here, in college?* Willow found
herself struggling with her response. "Growing up," she said,
"my parents constantly said 'You have to go to college. You have
to do better than I did.'" And Willow had. She'd taken her Narraguagus studies seriously—and had done well enough that her
grades, along with her family's lack of money, had garnered her
more than enough outside funding to cover her freshman-year
costs. "With all my scholarships and everything," she'd say,
with a look of disbelief, "they're giving me more money than
I need. I'm basically getting paid to go to college." But now, as
Willow considered her professor's question, she began to wonder whether four years at UMM would be worth her time. "I've
been trying to think more about who I am, and what I want to
do," she said. "Because, for so long I did what everyone else
wanted me to do."

So far, the UMM coursework hadn't posed much of a challenge for Willow. She'd felt a lot more pressure from the expectations Lee had placed on her at home. The more time she spent
with him, the more she realized that he was "basically like a
child." She'd found herself struggling to balance the demands of
"the house, my work outside school, and everything else that's
going on." Early on in their engagement, Willow would tell anyone who asked that Lee, a high school dropout, wanted the best
for her, that whenever she'd questioned the value of continuing
on with school, he'd urged her not to quit. From the start, Wil-

low said, "he encouraged me to go to the best school I could" if it meant getting a better degree. As a Narraguagus senior, she'd had the choice between UMM and the higher-ranked University of Maine at Presque Isle—four hours north of Lee's house. When she'd decided on UMM, "everyone assumed I was going there because I didn't want to leave Lee. But it wasn't that," Willow had told them. "It was that I wasn't ready to leave this area, this place. And I don't think I ever will be."

Still, Lee wasn't exactly making Willow's road to college completion easy. Every day, she cooked, cleaned, did her schoolwork, and catered to him. She stepped up her hours at the wharf, not just because she liked working there (although she did), but because somebody needed to make enough to pay the bills. Lee worked only occasionally, and what he made "wasn't enough to contribute anything." Before long, Willow had found herself paying for nearly all of her and Lee's needs, and "helping Lee's dad with the house bills too." And while there was no physical abuse, Lee exerted control over Willow in other ways. He "yelled all the time." He was quick to anger, whether at Willow, or simply upon encountering the slightest mishap. "He could stub his toe," said Willow, "and he could scream for hours." When, finally, Willow felt she could no longer endure Lee's outbursts—and the return to her past that they unleashed in her consciousness—she pleaded with him to stop. She told him she was suffering, that she couldn't sleep at night—and that when she did, she'd be awakened by nightmares of the worst moments with her dad. "Sometimes," said Willow, "when Lee would get mad, he'd turn to me and say, 'Why are you overreacting?' And I would tell him, 'I'm not overreacting. I'm reacting because I feel like I'm back, cornered, and my father is screaming at me again. But instead of him it's you.'"

Over time, Willow came to recognize the chokehold her family's dysfunction had placed on her, the way it followed her everywhere she went. She desperately wanted to leave it behind; she'd thought that, in her earliest days with Lee, perhaps she had. But the legacy of her childhood continued to pursue her at every turn. And the odds of escape were stacked against her.

Domestic abuse has haunted generations of families in the poorest and most rural parts of Maine, where experts agree that cases are underreported and victims' services are sparse. Even with underreporting, the numbers are unnerving. A 2016 survey found that Washington County had the highest percentage of interpersonal violence in the state. The county has only one domestic violence shelter, NextStep, with twelve beds in an undisclosed location. It also happens to be the only shelter of any kind in the county. Indeed, NextStep often fields calls from the homeless asking for a place to sleep. But the facility's funding only allows it to take in victims of abuse. "It's heartbreaking" to have to turn the homeless away, said NextStep associate director Kelly Brown. Headquartered in Machias and Ellsworth, NextStep's service area includes both Washington and Hancock Counties—a sweep of more than 4,000 square miles of non–Native American land. In 2018, nearly 50 percent of the nine hundred–plus people it served came from Washington County— even though Washington County represents only 10 percent of the consolidated two-county population.

With lobstering as the predominant Downeast Washington County industry, added Brown, "so many of the women we see from that area come from fishing households." Most live on large tracts of family land (owned by their husbands), and their abutting neighbors are often the parents, siblings, or extended relatives of their husbands. Because fishing brings in decent money, many of the victims are told by their husbands not to work, and they often don't have a car of their own. These, said Brown, are just some of the patterns of control that abusive men in rural Downeast homesteads exert over their victims. "Typically," she observed, "the victims don't know how to escape. They can't tell anyone, they have no transportation, and they have no income." As a result, NextStep estimates that less than one-quarter of those who are being abused in the area are finding their way to the facility. Isolated and alone, these women share an unspoken bond with Willow's mom. Ultimately, Lily had escaped the worst by leaving William, but not before she and her three children were scarred.

As Willow marked the start of her third year with Lee, the couple's relationship grew more strained. Lee had become increasingly controlling. He "was constantly checking my phone, and I wasn't allowed to see my friends." At one point, when Willow mentioned she might take a trip with a girlfriend, Lee forbade her. Things spiraled downward, to a point where the pair "was fighting all the time." Willow often found herself crying. She put on weight, and took less care of herself. And she searched desperately for an outlet to help ease her pain. She knew she could always turn to Vivian. But Vivian was facing her own challenges, and Willow didn't want to rest her burdens on her.

In the end, it was another old confidant—a boyfriend from Willow's grammar school days—who helped Willow escape. Willow was in fifth grade when she and Robert "dated," although they never physically met. Robert lived with his family in Michigan. He and Willow first encountered each other when a mutual gaming friend connected them through Minecraft. They became friends first, then dated virtually for nearly a year. In that time, Willow confided in Robert perhaps more than anyone other than Vivian. She found in him a kind and willing listener, and even from a distance of a thousand miles, the pair felt a mutual attraction. Although they'd ended their childhood romance, they continued to have feelings for each other. "But we were also still learning about ourselves," said Willow, "and though we talked off and on" for a while after the breakup, it had become "a sore subject." As Willow moved through her middle school years, there was a period when she and Robert stopped talking. "He was in high school," Willow recalled, "and I was going into high school, and we were both changing. And we didn't know how to do that together, because we were so young." In time, Willow and Robert moved past their uncertainty. They reclaimed their friendship, and eased into a pattern of regular contact—messaging and video chatting even after Willow and Lee had gotten engaged.

In those later years, Robert remained Willow's stalwart. He was someone with whom she could laugh and let her guard down, even in her most trying times. And although Willow had recounted to Lee the misery she'd endured as a child, she felt a gap in understanding from him. Robert helped fill that gap, perhaps because he was "actually there when it was happening." He knew "about Dad's heroin addiction when it was going on. He got to see how I was. I could be listening to a certain type of music, and he'd know what mood I was in, and what to say to fix everything."

Willow began to see the contrast between the two men in her life. As Robert cradled Willow, albeit without ever being in the same room with her, Lee "would just get pissed because I didn't want to speak, or because I was crying."

Still, it was not until Willow's troubles with Lee had reached a near breaking point that the spark of romance rekindled between Willow and Robert. One day, in the summer before Willow's freshman year at UMM, Willow and Lee had hit a low point. "We'd gotten in another fight," she recalled. "He was miserable, because his mom and dad had split up that spring, and he was taking his anger out on me." Willow and Robert were video chatting when Robert asked, "Why are you always so sad? You don't laugh as much as you used to. You don't talk about the same stuff you used to talk about." Willow began to open up to Robert about all she'd been going through—the anxiety and depression that had built up inside her, the way she constantly felt watched and overwhelmed. It didn't take long before Willow realized how much of herself she'd cast aside since moving in with Lee. And she resolved to break away.

From that point forward, what little remained of Willow's love for Lee lay in shards in a corner of their kitchen floor. Then came Robert's plea. *Come visit me in Michigan. Let's try this out and see where it might lead.* And the pair began to weave a dream. It flourished through texts and video chats, and bloomed into a plan for Willow to move to Michigan as soon as she finished her college degree. At first, Willow had explored the possibility that Robert might instead come east. She'd tested the waters by asking, "Would you move here, or would I move there?" Robert, who was working as a mechanic with his dad and lived in the comfort of his parents' home, had responded that he wasn't prepared to leave his life. To make things work, it would be up to Willow to leave hers. So in the end, she didn't really have any choice in the matter.

And yet Willow convinced herself that this was the path she was meant to take, even though she'd be walking away from the only place she'd ever known, a place she'd always held close to her heart. "My whole life, I've never wanted to leave," said Willow. "I love it down here. But I need to start over. I need to not have everyone know my father was that heroin addict, and that I don't speak to my other side of the family, and everything else. And I could have that there."

Vivian watched Willow's newest chapter unfold from afar, with a combination of hope and concern. She knew Willow's gambit was risky. But a big part of her was rooting for the couple to thrive, at least for the moment—for, if nothing else, it would put an end to Willow's catastrophe with Lee. Vivian even offered to join Willow on her planned summer road trip to Michigan. Vivian had recognized early on the damage that Lee's controlling ways had inflicted upon her best friend. She'd become all too familiar with the patterns of Willow and Lee's relationship—in Willow's past, and in her own. And although she maintained a healthy skepticism over the wisdom of Willow's latest course correction, she'd stick by Willow just as she always had, and just as Willow had always done for her.

Months would pass before Willow worked up the courage to leave Lee. Indeed, the end was triggered by Lee himself. He'd found messages from Robert on Willow's phone, and he'd "flipped out." He kept asking, "Why?" And Willow would respond, "I don't look at you as a boyfriend anymore, or a fiancé. I look at you as a brother, or a kid I take care of all the time." Even so, Lee pleaded with Willow to stay, then finally turned to her and said, "It's Robert or me." And Willow responded, "I choose me."

As Willow prepared to leave, she felt a rush of sadness for her ex-fiancé, especially when she thought about how much he cared for, and would miss, her beloved Eeyore. She told Lee he could hold on to Eeyore for a bit, so that he might give the dog a proper goodbye. But Lee was angry, and hurt, and as Willow made her offer, he grabbed Eeyore and put him in his car and drove away. He told Willow that the only way she'd get Eeyore back was by calling the police. So Willow "called the cops, and they said they couldn't do anything." Willow and Lee had been together for so long that, technically, Eeyore was "a piece of property"—like a chair or table they might wrestle over as they divvied up the things they'd shared.

That night, alone in her dad's house, Willow couldn't stop crying, for all she'd given and withstood—and for her beloved dog. Early the next morning, Willow arose to a remorseful text from Lee. He told her he was sorry, and urged her to come and collect Eeyore. His only request was to wait until his dad got up, so that he might say goodbye.

A few hours later, when Willow arrived at the house that she and Lee had shared, she hugged Lee's dad and said, "I'm sorry."

He answered, with a slightly puzzled look, "What are you sorry about?"

And Willow said, "I'm leaving."

"Please don't," Lee's dad began.

But Willow stopped him and said, "I just can't do it anymore."

And he responded, "No . . . I know. I've watched it." And there wasn't much more that he could say.

Weeks later, after things had settled down, after a bit of cooling off and taking stock, Lee and Willow found a wider ledge on which to land their history. "We still talk," said Willow, "and I take Eeyore to see him every once in a while." But in the end, no matter what the future brought, Willow knew that by leaving she'd taken a step toward doing right by herself. "I needed to go," she said. "I needed to do something with my life."

Chapter 14

Searching

In the fall of her freshman year, Vivian arrived at UMO with the optimism of a child. As her time at Narraguagus had drawn to a close, she had tasted the possibility of life beyond Harrington. She looked back on how far she'd traveled since she'd first arrived at the high school—how much energy it had taken to drop her mask, to walk away from the pickup trucks, the social media obsessions, and the skin-tight jeans and camo shirts that distinguished the cool kids. And how relieved she'd been when she'd finally done it. When it came to academics, she'd kept her head about her, even as her adventures beyond the school grounds persisted. She'd graduated third in her high school class and had chosen UMO largely because it was her parents' alma mater and the top pick of smart local kids who choose not to stray too far. She'd begun to distance herself from the church, while holding on to her belief in something bigger than herself. And she'd laid out a plan to study biology, because writing doesn't pay the bills.

In the blink of an eye, November came. With each week's progression, Vivian found herself counting the hours until Friday afternoon, when she could drive two hours north to Houlton to spend two glorious days with Andy. It would be her ninth such trip since she'd arrived at UMO nearly three months earlier. Now, Vivian picked at her chicken tenders in a corner booth at the Bear's Den Lounge, and worried out loud about the snowstorm that threatened to derail her plans. If she couldn't get out early enough, she might be stuck in Orono for the weekend. There were worse fates than this, but right now, Vivian couldn't imagine one.

Vivian swept her arm toward the darkening campus. "It's so impersonal here," she lamented. "I can't even get into my building unless I have my keycard." With its 2,200-person freshman class, UMO was a far cry from Narraguagus. At Vivian's high school graduation, she'd stood with forty-four classmates, seventeen of whom she'd known since kindergarten. For years, she had felt stifled by the smallness of Harrington and fantasized about life beyond its clutches. But now, Vivian felt alone. "People see things differently here," she said. "I've made one friend, but we're not close. I don't go to a lot of my classes. The food makes my stomach hurt, because it's horrible. The water makes my stomach hurt, because it's city water." She hadn't yet fallen into a deep-rooted depression. "Not like before." But Vivian knew that if she didn't find a way out of Orono, she'd spiral downward.

A few days earlier, Vivian had submitted her application for transfer to the University of Maine at Fort Kent, some two hundred miles north of Orono, just shy of the Canadian border crossing on the far north crown of Maine. It's a rural school, with a 52-acre campus and an undergraduate student body of fewer than two thousand. Most Mainers also view it as less competitive than UMO. Vivian knew that some might look askance at her decision, but she made it a practice not to put much stock in what other people thought. She just wanted to be in a place where she could "be outside, learn about agriculture, and be hands on."

Indeed, Fort Kent had beckoned Vivian for quite a while. It had been her school of choice when she'd first applied to colleges, but her dad, Max, had other ideas. Orono blood runs deep in the Westford family: Max, his brother, and his UMO-valedictory sister were all alums. Vivian's parents met and started dating there. Despite all that, though, Vivian knew her mom would understand her desire to break free. Indeed, from the moment Vivian had made the decision to attend UMO, Emma had expressed concern that it might be wrong for her. Telling Emma about her plans to transfer might be a relief to both of them—and further evidence that mother and daughter were like-minded and like-spirited. But her dad. That was another story. Vivian struggled to build up the courage to break her news to him. Vivian worried, too, that Max would chafe at the limits the five-hour drive from Fort Kent to Harrington would place on Vivian's trips home. Vivian decided that her best course of action with Max was to confide first in her stepmother, Caroline. In turn, Caroline would come to Vivian's rescue. She'd work on Max, and make it okay.

Back at UMO, Vivian continued to drown in the sea of her discomfort. Aside from hating the food, the water, the size, and the academics, Vivian bristled at the student culture. A couple of years before Vivian had arrived at UMO, the school had introduced tuition matching for surrounding northeast states, with the hope of boosting enrollments in the face of Maine's aging population. Now, kids from Connecticut, Massachusetts, New Hampshire, and Vermont could attend Orono for the same amount they'd pay to attend a public university at home. The strategy had worked. In the first year of the policy change, out-of-state freshman commitments had increased by more than 50 percent, shrinking Mainers' presence to about half the incoming class. Deposits from Massachusetts alone had spiked more than 80 percent. Vivian found the trend troubling, and unfair to Maine residents like her. She lamented the influx of people "with radical ideas" who were "turning Maine into a blue state," and saw Orono as a place that was far more liberal than it used to be. A self-described conservative, Vivian contended, "I'm not a politically charged person, but this is a politically charged campus. Everybody is pushing you to join the protest." Students here, to Vivian, were also "very urbanized. Their mindset is just, 'Eat people alive.'" But, she added, "It's not their fault. They've grown up like that. They don't know a different world."

Vivian hadn't tried to seek out conservative classmates at Orono, but she also hadn't stumbled on any. Instead, whenever she felt isolated, she looked to her parents for perspective. "They're both conservatives, and my dad has gotten even more conservative since he's gone back to being a town selectman." Vivian and Max were aligned on most issues. "I'm pro-life, pro-NRA, and I lean conservatively on taxes," she said. "I want to see more economic equality, but you can't have a state if you're under water." Still, father and daughter sometimes clashed. "I told my dad the other day, 'Tell me that humans don't contribute to global warming one more time and I'll freak out. I'll freaking lose my crap on you.' I mean, polar bears dying, glaciers melting, the whole Chicken Little thing, it's real. I'm conservative, but I also believe in science."

Vivian and Max also continued to wrestle with fallout from the previous year's marriage of Vivian's cousin Ben, who is gay.

Ben was "like a brother" to Vivian. He'd come out five years earlier, when he was twenty-three. In response, much of the extended Westford family had refused to attend his wedding. "It was a big divider," recalled Vivian, who did attend. "And it was really, really hurtful to Ben." Things had improved slightly between Ben and other family members since the wedding. "We took family pictures the other day," said Vivian, "and Ben came to those. But then we had dinner at my house, and he didn't come." Vivian knew that Ben hadn't forgiven Max and Caroline for the letter they'd written when they received his wedding invitation. In it, said Vivian, they'd "expressed their distaste," and declined to attend. Vivian struggled to come to terms with this aspect of Max and Caroline's faith, the way it had moved them to reject Ben's path. "I guess it was their form of love for him, in a different way," she reflected. "It was the only thing that they knew to do." Sometime after the wedding, Max had reached out to Ben and his husband. They'd started talking, but the relationship remained strained. Vivian wasn't sure if it would ever be fully reconciled.

Come late December, Vivian was at her mother's home in Harrington, packing for the journey north to Fort Kent. Lately, she'd been thinking a lot about her past. Her entire life, she'd struggled to feel comfortable with those around her. "The people Downeast aren't like me, the people at Orono aren't like me. And I've always felt . . . set apart." When Vivian had started dating Andy two years earlier, and had spent time in Houlton, she'd begun to feel, for the first time, like she belonged. "When I go up north," she said, "I have friends. I finally feel like I'm home." Thinking about the contrast to Downeast, she added, "I'm not above it, I'm just different. I wasn't going to be happy with a boy from my area. They're either super nerdy or uncultured—or, if they're good guys that you feel really comfortable with, they're gay. I wanted a conservative Maine boy, but I didn't want a Downeast mentality." People from Harrington, especially those from the older generations, "pride themselves on working hard, on putting their money into their homes, and that's good. But I worry that they're not learning. They're not growing. There's a contentment, a closed-off feeling that they embrace. I want more. I still want to learn."

As Vivian looked toward the future, her voice floated with excitement. "I'm really hopeful that the people are better at Fort Kent, more open, and more down to earth than at UMO," she said. "I don't care what their views are, but you just gotta give me something. And I think a slower, more personal environment will be better for my state of mind. Because until now I've been isolated. *So* isolated. To the point where it's painful to go about my day."

So it was that Vivian Westford, pride of Harrington, left for the farthest reaches of the U.S. border—Fort Kent, Maine, population approximately 4,000—to escape isolation. For Vivian, physical isolation wasn't the problem. It was the personal isolation that needed to be overcome.

Chapter 15

Moneyball

It was 11:00 a.m. on a Sunday. Mckenna, now well into her senior year at Narraguagus, was practicing pitches with her long-time trainer, Jed Peters. Nine other girls were there too, drilling across the brightly lit Ellsworth Elementary School gym. This was Mckenna's routine, nearly every Sunday, ten months a year. On this particular morning, Mckenna was going full bore, trying to perfect her rise ball. She moved through her paces with grit and determination, her blood-red muscle T resting gently against her torso, her waist-length hair packed tightly atop her head. Two weeks earlier, she'd clocked her fastball at 64 miles per hour. She'd been battling to hit 65 ever since.

Jed moved with ease among the girls. He stopped to watch Mckenna. "Rise ball? That's a rise drop," he teased. Mckenna's boyfriend, Ethan, and her mom, Phoebe, looked on from the bleachers, as Mckenna and Jed settled into a familiar banter.

Jed grinned, and said, "I need to watch a couple. That means you have to pitch."

Mckenna gave him a hard stare, wound her pitch, and the ball dropped low.

"What is our goal here?" he asked. "What are we looking for the hitter to do? Strike out, or what? Pop up."

Jed watched Mckenna pitch a few more in. As she struggled to find the right arc and let the ball get away, Jed yelled, with a lilt in his voice, "That's the *home run* ball."

It was midwinter, and all in all, Mckenna couldn't complain about the year she'd recently left behind. Back in the spring of 2018, people had begun to talk about a powerful junior pitcher from Downeast Washington County. Mckenna Holt, they said, was worth a second look. She had a mean fastball, and was averaging more than ten strikeouts a game. She was a difference-maker for the talented Narraguagus squad—helping the Lady Knights go 18-1 in regular play. In the postseason, the team had advanced through four tournament rounds to face Madison High for the state title. The Lady Knights were jubilant. It was only the second time in Narraguagus history that the girls' softball squad had made it that far. But Mckenna knew that Madison would be a tough opponent; they hadn't lost a game all season.

In June, the two teams met for the championship game at St. Joseph's College, just outside of Portland, and some three hours south of Harrington. By midday, the temperature had crept into the eighties, and the sun beat hot against the bleachers as the girls took to the field. The traveling hometown crowd wasn't nearly as big as the one that had gathered in Augusta two years earlier for the Narraguagus girls' basketball win. But the softball squad's fans made plenty of noise to make up for their numbers. *Wouldn't it be wonderful*, they said to each other, *to place that Gold Glove in the Narraguagus trophy case next to the 2016 girls' Gold Ball?*

When the game began, the Lady Knights came out roaring. They scored three quick runs in the top of the first inning. The Madison Bulldogs responded with one in the bottom of the first. Then, just as quickly, things started to unravel. In the second inning, the Lady Knights went down swinging. As Mckenna took to the mound, she looked shaky. She hadn't yet found her groove. A wild pitch and a stolen base helped the Bulldogs score one run early in the bottom of the second. Two outs followed. Then came the unrecoverable blow: a three-run double that gave the Bulldogs a 5–3 lead. In the end, Madison took the title, 7–3, with a two-hitter for the Bulldogs' ace pitcher. After the game, Mckenna quietly told the local press, "It was unlucky for us. I knew I hadn't quite hit my spot yet, but I settled in afterward pretty good. We just couldn't get our bats going again."

The loss felt like a punch in the gut to Mckenna. She let the feeling sit for a moment, but just as quickly pushed it away. Mckenna could see her future, and she was certain there'd be plenty of wins ahead.

True to her prediction, as the spring of 2019 drew closer, despite her ankle and basketball setbacks, Mckenna was feeling good about pretty much everything in her life. Her grades were holding steady. Her relationship with Ethan was solid. Her pitching was on track. She'd recently been presented with a Daughters of the American Revolution Good Citizens Award for "dependability, service, leadership, and patriotism." Around here, those types of accolades were treasured. What's more, Mckenna had learned that both UMM and Bangor-based Husson University had granted her admission for the coming fall. Husson's varsity softball pitching coach had even sent her a letter of interest, all but offering a starting spot on the team. Then, two weeks later, the coach resigned. Husson had since tapped Jed Peters to replace her, and he said he'd "love to get Mckenna" into Husson's lineup. But Mckenna wasn't jumping. The lure of fishing was top of mind, and a brand-new lobster boat was calling her name.

Indeed, Mckenna and her dad had twice made the thirty-mile drive from Harrington to Winter Harbor to examine the boat. They'd liked what they'd seen, and they were closing in on an offer. The vessel was one foot longer and four feet wider than the *River Rodent*, the 26-footer that had been handed down to Mckenna by her older brothers. It wouldn't come cheap—it would set Mckenna back about $50,000. She'd be making three payments a year, at $2,300 or so a pop, for a long time to come. Still, it would be worth the stretch, and Mckenna felt confident she'd be able to make the payments work. She'd just come off a strong fishing season, and she felt ready to step things up. She'd earned $20,000 fishing part time from April through November, and had done it with the 150 traps her student license had allowed. Phoebe, who knew the numbers inside out, calculated that, with the 300-trap latitude of a newly obtained commercial license, Mckenna could make three times more if she lobstered full time at full capacity after she graduated.

Phoebe and Jake had insisted for years that Mckenna get a college degree. But every so often they wondered if it really made sense—especially when they saw the drive with which their daughter fished. The question of college was something so many of Phoebe and Jake's friends struggled with, and it wasn't an easy call. Most Downeast families who owned their boats and took hauling seriously made enough money to be financially secure. The most successful fishing families had funds to spare, even after the considerable expense of buying, maintaining, and running their boats. Many of them poured sizable sums of money, for these parts, into their homes. They bought the latest model pickup trucks, smartphones, and recreational vehicles for their teenage kids, and contributed generously to local causes. They sat at the top of the social pecking order, and dominated local civic leadership posts. And these days, with lobstering in a boom phase, returns were particularly good. This was one key reason more and more girls like Mckenna were opting to fish.

But the Holts and their neighbors knew that good times can easily turn bad. Older Downeast generations had seen enough boom-and-bust cycles to not get too cocky about the current lobster bonanza. Here, as elsewhere across rural America, the dangers of relying too heavily on one industry were etched in the frames of shuttered Main Street storefronts.

Cherryfield, a historic village, stood as a case in point. If today you were to stop in at the Cherryfield library and stumble upon a certain local historian whose husband's roots trace back to Cherryfield's late eighteenth-century settlers, she'll gladly regale you with the full-color version of Cherryfield's saga. As she tells it, Cherryfield once was a Downeast jewel. A flourishing lumber center, the town had nine dams along the Narraguagus River, each with up to three working mills that helped move twelve to fifteen million feet of timber a year. But by 1920, most of the timber was gone, along with hundreds of residents who migrated to western states to chase the lumber. They never returned. Pulp production, then blueberry farming, moved in to take timber's place, but neither brought the prosperity that once graced Cherryfield. The "upper-crust families" of the town's heyday, who'd lived in grand homes on the ridge and had sent their children to Ivy League schools, were largely replaced by working-class immigrants (many from Ireland), who settled there for steady mill jobs. The descendants of those immigrants form the backbone of Cherryfield life today.

By the 1970s, Cherryfield's population had dropped from its turn-of-the-century peak of two thousand to fewer than nine hundred. Along with the human exodus went the five grocery stores, motel, restaurant, barber shop, beauty salon, furniture store, hardware store, and Ford dealership that had once thrived on Main Street. The generation that had grown up beneath the clamor of the water mills was all but gone. The river that runs through the heart of town stood cold and still.

The lobster fishermen who dominated the nearby towns of Harrington and Milbridge lived with the specter of Cherryfield's cautionary tale. They knew they should encourage their kids to pursue a solid backup plan—and they'd been told, time and again, that a college degree was "necessary" in this day and age. *But necessary for what?*, many would ask. *And at what cost?*

Indeed, many fishing families were hesitant to push their kids toward a high-priced four-year college degree—particularly at a liberal arts school. They were skeptical that what the kids would learn there would be of much use when they returned home. Local school administrators tended to agree. While they generally encouraged kids to pursue some form of higher education (as well as the popular option of military service), they bemoaned the fact that no other county in Maine but theirs lacked a full-fledged career and technical educational (CTE) center. Narraguagus did offer vocational classes for nurse's assistant (CNA) training and law enforcement. And twenty minutes away, Machias had long been dubbed the area's CTE center—but its offerings were limited to the culinary and building trades.

The history of how Narraguagus's CNA program—a bright spot in the area's training efforts—had originally gotten started highlighted local parents' yearning for more practical career pathways for their kids. The district leadership had long appealed to the state for help in starting, and funding, those path-ways—to no avail. Finally, in 2012, thanks in large part to Lauren Donovan's persistence, the district's leadership decided to launch a CNA offering on its own. The move would result in a tax increase for residents, but as Lauren recalled, the community was "so supportive of anything that gives kids an opportunity for employable skills during their high school career" that "no one questioned it."

Despite the program's near-instant popularity, it would take nearly three years for district leaders to persuade the state to recognize and help pay for it. In the end, their persistence yielded dividends. Students who completed the coursework and were certified (all but one who have done so are girls) had a good chance of finding work at a nearby Milbridge-based nursing home—and, if so motivated, to parlay their earnings and experience into higher-level studies for better-paying nursing jobs. Still, those seeking vocational options beyond those offered at Narraguagus and Machias faced daily hour-long bus rides to the closest full-blown CTE center in Ellsworth. Once there, some students would then board a second bus, for another half hour, to reach a satellite location in Bucksport or Mount Desert Island.

All that began to change in the fall of 2018, when the local school superintendent—with Lauren's full engagement and support—led the effort by four Downeast school districts to secure state funds to build a locally based CTE center. The group beat out more than a dozen applicants from other Maine counties to win a two-million-dollar grant. Residents Downeast cheered the news. For years, they'd been clamoring for additional vocational opportunities. They knew there was plenty of room for more boatbuilders and diesel mechanics to meet the needs of the thriving fishing industry. There was demand, too, for more early childhood educators. And those examples, said locals, only scratched the surface of what might be possible. With a center of their own—which would ultimately be sited at a former super-market in the town of Columbia—Downeast's least fortunate families saw a chance for their kids to climb out of poverty. The more successful lobstering families, like Mckenna's, saw an op-portunity for their kids to opt into a low-cost, practical plan B.

Americans overwhelmingly see value in technical and skill-based education for high schoolers. A 2017 Phi Delta Kappan poll found more than 80 percent support for "job or career skills classes, even if that means students might spend less time in academic classes"—and nearly 90 percent support for schools to "offer certificate or licensing programs that qualify students for employment in a given field." Yet, even though nearly all schools in America offer some form of CTE programming, rural areas face more participation barriers than cities—with longer distances to travel for training sites, fewer work-based learning activities, and less mentoring by local employers and on-the-job training in the form of internships, clinicals, practicums, and the like. In Maine, and certainly in Downeast Washington County, the deficit in this arena has long been apparent, with the clear exception of lobster-fishing apprenticeships.

In the summer of 2020, Lauren Donovan was named director of the newly configured Coastal Washington County Institute of Technology—and in September, the Columbia-based facility opened its doors with diesel, auto, early childhood, and weld-ing programs for local high schoolers, and an adult ed class for welding. These programs, along with the addition of aquama-rine studies in nearby Jonesport, would bring the total number of nearby CTE offerings to nine—spread across four locations. In building out the new site, Lauren and her team hoped to centralize better opportunities for local students. "The plan is to expand options in Columbia, and perhaps to move some of the other programs to this site," said Lauren.

It was nearly noon, and Mckenna's pitching practice was coming to a close. Jed Peters stepped to the center of the gym. "It's time for Moneyball," he yelled, and the girls fell in line. Forty-three feet away, the standard distance from home plate to the softball mound, Jed placed a ball on a batting tee. He slipped a ten-dollar bill beneath the ball. It was a familiar game to Jed's protégées: knock the ball clean off the tee with a pitch, and the money's yours. If no one prevails, Jed adds more money to the pot. Mckenna, who was first to pitch, was loose and confident. She was on a three-week Moneyball winning streak, and she had her sights set on another victory. But Mckenna's ball drifted, as did the balls of the pitchers who followed.

As Jed moved to round two, slipping a five-dollar bill beneath the ten, Mckenna yelled, "More."

He echoed, "More?" and added another ten.

From the bleachers, Phoebe quipped, "She's not bashful when it comes to money," and Jed nodded and laughed.

The pot was up to twenty-five dollars. Mckenna stepped up and grazed the ball. It teetered, settled back onto the tee, and hung on in the face of the nine remaining girls. Mckenna was back for her final try, and she nailed it. As the ball flew off the tee, it swiped the side of Jed's mouth, nearly knocking out a couple of his teeth. And Mckenna smiled.

Chapter 16

Soaring

Josie was content. Just before Christmas, she'd boarded a bus from New Haven to Bangor, making her way back from Yale to Harrington for winter break. Except for a slightly bumpy initiation into Chinese language, Josie's first semester at Yale had been, by all accounts, a success. The final days of December had brought the Dekkers' usual feast of family time: Christmas Eve services together at Harrington's Lighthouse Baptist Church; morning gifts at home; a celebratory dinner at Grammy Mae and Pappy Stuart's farmhouse; and a straight-shot twelve-hour drive early the next morning to Grandma Liza and Grandpa Noah's in Brockville, Ontario. By the time the Dekkers had returned from Canada a few days later, all Josie wanted to do was decompress in the comfort of her own home, and take stock of the whirlwind she'd experienced since September.

Josie knew that, by making it to Yale, she'd beaten the Downeast odds. She'd been the second student ever admitted there from Narraguagus High; her eldest sister, Angela, had been the first. Nor were Josie and Angela the only Dekkers to rise to the top among their Downeast peers. Elizabeth, the second born, was a dancer and premed student, on scholarship at the University of Utah. Katherine, the youngest—whom Josie described as the "most purely brilliant" of the four—routinely turned teachers' heads and was poised to match, or perhaps even exceed, her sisters' successes. Angela, Katherine, and Josie had all been valedictorians at Narraguagus. They were the ones the college guidance counselor placed at the top of every list.

By late January, after her happy time at home, Josie was back on campus. She wasted little time sorting out her spring-semester schedule. She knew exactly which courses she wanted to take: Sculpture, Modern Architecture, Microeconomics, a continuation of Chinese, and her "instant favorite," a seminar called Divine Law and Historical Perspectives. The seminar would be Josie's first foray into reading the Bible as an academic text—to be poked at and prodded, not simply heeded. It would also mark the first time she'd hear non-Christian peers talk about their faiths. The class, taught by the head of the Religious Studies department, had six students: one Muslim, two Jewish, two Christian, and one nonpracticing. After the first session, Josie had already begun to consider her own background from the outside, looking in. She'd always known she came from "a culturally Christian area, where, even though a lot of people don't practice Christianity, if you ask anyone, they'll say 'I'm a Christian.'" She'd long recognized that there was a "generally accepted set of ideas in the community, rooted in Christianity, that our social values are centered around." But until now, she hadn't explored "from a different vantage point, what those values represent."

Josie found meaning in those explorations, even as her Christian faith remained a constant in her life. She kept that faith honed, spending Mondays and Wednesdays at Yale Gospel Choir rehearsal, Tuesdays at Bible Study, Thursdays at the weekly Yale Students for Christ (YSC) meeting, and Sundays worshipping at the nearby Ridge Street Baptist Church. In these ways, Josie remained true to the core of her upbringing, much like her sister Angela had before her.

As an undergraduate, Angela had made a strong connection with YSC, the local chapter of Campus Crusade for Christ—so much so that she'd returned to work there after graduation. Angela had embraced other aspects of Yale too, especially those that nourished her body and soul. She'd led freshman outdoor orientation hiking trips, planted trees around New Haven through the school's Urban Resources Initiative, and advocated for refugees. But unlike Josie, Angela had steered clear of the party scene that dominated the university's residential college life. Yale's campus parties were unlike anything Angela had known back home. Downeast, kids didn't dress in gowns and tuxedos. They didn't set each other up on blind dates for formals. What's more, in high school, neither Angela nor Josie had been much into whatever social scene was going on Downeast. Josie was one of the few girls in her Narraguagus class who rarely dated—unlike most of the girls around her, she didn't have a boyfriend until senior year. She certainly didn't party with friends in the backwoods, or along the Sunrise Trail. And the only gown she owned, and packed for Yale, was her prom dress.

Things were different now. Josie embraced the excitement of campus formals. The thrill of putting on a new gown (even if it was borrowed from a suitemate), the energy of dancing in a decked-out ballroom, the half dread, half thrill of meeting the blind date her friends had paired her with for a dance—these were the bright lines between Josie's past and present. And when one party ended, Josie found herself looking forward to the next. In those moments, she wasn't tethered to her church upbringing. It was still her sustenance, but Yale's social scene was her dessert.

Back in Harrington, Josie and Angela's mother, Brianna, would reflect on what it was that distinguished the two sisters. After all, they'd grown up in the same home, with the same foundation of discipline and self-control, and the same adherence to church teachings. Both girls were whip smart—and, through their intellect, would instantly engage. Perhaps because she was the younger sister, who had not carried the burdens that eldest children so often do, Josie was more open and gregarious. Her touch was lighter, her smile lasted longer, and her self-effacing charm lingered. She also had the benefit of having followed Angela to the Ivy League, of having known for years, through her, what lay ahead. "I think it's easier for Josie," said Brianna. "I think it's always easier to do something when you've seen someone close to you do it first."

In the four years since Angela had arrived at Yale, the school had also worked to ease the transition for kids like Angela and Josie. It had stepped up efforts to recruit more low- and middle-income students, and to connect them to one another once they were admitted. In Josie's outdoor orientation trip, an intense six-day hike in New Hampshire's White Mountains, five of the seven in her group had grown up in small towns. In her seven-girl rooming suite, "almost everyone in the group had concerns about money." For students like Josie and her suitemates, the school's efforts to help out in small ways made a difference. There was money to buy rugs and furniture for the common areas in their rooming suites. Money to reimburse low-income kids for buying a laptop or printer, and to help meet the costs of joining a campus club. Money for internships and summer travel. All this on top of a financial aid policy that covered the full freight for students whose families earned $65,000 or less. Because Josie's dad had pulled in steady money with his roofing and construction work, the Dekkers had narrowly missed the zero-payment cutoff. Still, thanks to Yale's sliding scale policy, plus a handful of outside scholarships, Josie was on the hook for only $200 of the nearly $70,000 in first-year tuition, room, and board.

With Yale's latest push to help less advantaged kids, said Brianna, "I think the culture changed a little bit." She saw differences almost immediately in Josie's and Angela's experiences. For Josie, "if someone is going out to dinner and she can't afford it," she said, "or another person suggests someone else can't afford it, they say it. Angela can't remember anyone saying that her freshman year. There was a lot more stigma to being lower income. It's a striking difference in just four years."

Now, well into her first year, Josie felt good about how things were unfolding. She'd gotten her bearings, taken a deep breath, and begun to map out her future. She knew how quickly these four years would pass. She needed to be ready for life after Yale—and beyond her Downeast home. Her latest idea was to major in Art or Art History, pursue a Ph.D., and ultimately teach. The thought had taken hold one morning during her first months at Yale, when a teaching assistant stood in for Josie's art history professor. "This grad student walks in," said Josie. "She looks almost exactly like me, with long blond hair, and starts with, 'Hi, I'm Josie. I'll be teaching your class today.' And I just had this moment of 'I could do that. I would really, really like doing that.'" For days, the thought persisted. "I was still slightly hung up over the idea of going into politics, of thinking, 'I want to change the world.' But being here, I've seen that if you teach, and you can just touch a few people's lives at a time, they're going to touch more lives. So I realized, that's a way of changing the world too, maybe one of the most valuable ways." She'd also begun working on a summer plan, and she had her mind set on international travel. If all worked out, she'd soon be on a Greek island studying art and archaeology, with Yale covering nearly all her costs.

When Josie had been younger, she'd spent lots of time around ladders at her dad's worksites. As Dan climbed high to paint and patch and seal the roofs of weather-beaten Cherryfield homes, Josie would stare up in wonder. She was fearful of heights—but as she grew, she took it as a challenge to make her way to one of those ladder's highest rungs. She'd climbed upward, bit by bit, pausing at each rung to steady her weight. When she'd finally made it to the top, she peered across the tips of Downeast's formidable trees and imagined her future. Whatever was out there—that was what she wanted. All it would take was a few more tasks, a little more grit, and another round of prayers.

Now, Josie thought about how far she'd traveled since those adolescent summer days. She was more conscious of her Baptist background, and more inclined to examine it. She was not ready to abandon her roots, but she felt in her heart that she needed to expand them. She was still intensely tied to family, but less so to the Downeast land on which her grandparents had staked their claim. She would not work the Downeast soil as they had; she would not nurture her dreams upon it. She had released herself from her hometown, in part because she'd been able to reach high enough to grab the top rung. And as Josie stood on that higher perch, she realized there was more to this view than she'd ever imagined.

All she had to do was hang on tight and keep her balance.

Part Four

The Way Life Should Be

Chapter 17

Powered by Lobsters

Not long after Mckenna had wrapped up her first season of full-time fishing, she met Olivia and Brady Marshall for a late-morning lunch. They sat in a back booth at 44 North, one of two full-service restaurants in Milbridge. After the summer season, it's the only place to eat in town that's open past midafternoon. Mckenna's white Ford F-150 Lariat was parked just outside. Mckenna had bought the pickup truck—sticker price over forty thousand dollars—as a high school junior, with money she'd earned from fishing. The truck was unmistakably hers: A massive green and black decal on the rear window bore her new boat's name, *F/V Spittin' Image*, and the license plate frame read "Powered by Lobsters."

Christmas was five days away, and the restaurant was nearly full. The air outside was crisp, and the mood inside was buoyant. A hearty middle-aged waitress with a broad smile and full face raced to and from the kitchen to check which offerings from the crowded menu were still available. The place was about to close for two weeks, and food options were dwindling.

Olivia sat across from Mckenna, who made room for Brady as he slid alongside her.

"Well," said Olivia, "we've had better seasons."

Mckenna nodded. This year, fishing up the river had been tough. Ironically, although climatologists in recent years have warned that warming gulf waters might ultimately spell trouble for the thriving Maine lobster industry, inshore fishermen like Mckenna and Olivia worried more about the persistence of cold-water temperatures well into their summer fishing season. For Mckenna, who fished "new shell" lobsters, cold waters often meant empty traps. That's because, in order to grow, lobsters need to shed their exoskeleton—to molt—in summer months. Water temperature affects this process; the colder the waters, the longer the new shell takes to harden. And without the protection of a shell for the weeks it takes to grow a new one, molted lobsters will hide, making them elusive to fishermen.

"At least the guys offshore are doing all right," Olivia added, motioning to Brady. "So hopefully, for us, he's makin' up for it."

Long, thick layers of blond hair framed the angles of Olivia's profile. A thin line of black eyeliner punctuated her blue eyes.

"Seemed like the lobsters held off offshore a little bit," said Olivia. "They were like, 'Okay, we gotta crawl in a hole here to shed right off.' And they didn't make it into the river, basically."

Mckenna nodded again, as though she couldn't blame the lobsters for steering clear of the frigid waters. "It felt like it would never warm up," she said. "Sean Lawton came down under the boat in the middle of July to cut rope out of my wheel, and there he was, puttin' on his dry suit, with an insulated thing, to do it."

"Usually in July they can just cut the rope out in their underwear," said Olivia.

"Yep. But there he was, just standing at the boat with his dry suit looking down at the water," Mckenna continued, "and I'm like, 'Sean, it *can't* be that cold.' And he's like, 'I don't know. It's pretty cold.' So I say to him, 'Let me have that dry suit, and I'll go down and cut the rope myself.'"

Brady and Olivia laughed knowingly. That was Mckenna, all right.

There was no doubt that the 2019 season had begun slowly. But Mckenna had pushed on, and had upped her efforts as the river warmed. She certainly didn't waste time complaining. Talk didn't bring more lobsters up from their holes, and it didn't get them hoisted into her traps. Mckenna knew from experience: the best thing she could do was put her head down and put in the work.

Now, at the season's close, Mckenna's perseverance had paid off. She'd made strong hauls, and earned good money to show for them. True, she'd ended up with fewer pounds of catch than last year for every haul—but that had been the case this season for fishermen up and down the Maine coast. The state's early cold snap had packed a wallop, helping push haul totals down by nearly 20 percent. But demand had been steady, and by summer's peak, the average price per pound had soared to a record high. In the end, Maine's lobster prices had landed an average of 20 percent higher than in 2018.

As for Mckenna, she'd pulled in thirty thousand dollars for the year. After she backed out her costs, most of which went to bait, she'd cleared two-thirds of her earnings. Twenty thousand net wasn't bad at all, reflected Mckenna, "because I really didn't fish that hard." Between schoolwork and playing soccer for UMM, she said, "I only fished a couple of days a week, and I was still doing really good compared to some of the guys that were fishin' a lot more than I was." Mckenna added, after a moment of thought, "It was pretty successful for hardly even workin,' it felt like."

If only that damn herring hadn't been so expensive, Mckenna figured, she'd have cleared a lot more. A herring shortage had hit the region hard, and prices had skyrocketed of late. Fishermen had begun experimenting with other types of bait, just to avoid hemorrhaging money to keep their traps going, but everyone knew that nothing beat herring. "For a while," said Mckenna, "herring was the cheapest option. When I first started fishing, I was only paying forty bucks a tray. Then, this year, I started at eighty bucks. And now I'm paying a hundred and five a tray." Even at that price, Mckenna was one of the luckier ones. She was able to get a steady flow of herring from her brother Matthew's sideline business. With that, said Mckenna, "I've had plenty of bait. And I've been mixing it up too—using herring and pig hide" to make it go further.

An hour into lunch with Olivia and Brady, Mckenna was so wrapped up in conversation that she'd barely made a dent in her chicken Alfredo. She nudged the tangle into a take-home box, as talk turned to lobster-boat racing. It was no shock to any-one that Olivia had again posted top numbers this racing season. The previous summer, in her debut effort, Olivia had swept the competition. Now, she'd ended her second season with a 10-1 record. Both years, she'd taken gold in her boat category. As for her single loss this season, Olivia was quick to flag it. "I actu-ally won all my points races, so I'm considered undefeated in my class. And the guy that beat me blew his engine out," she said with a laugh.

"But he'll be rebuilt this year—and stronger—so be careful," warned Brady.

"Yeah, he probably will be," said Olivia. "Fact is, this year I'm expecting a little bit different. After a couple of years of winning, you get a target on your back, and I'm feeling it."

"There's a lot of competition," Brady agreed. "And it's gettin' stronger. Every year is gettin' bigger."

"Yep," said Mckenna. "It seems like racing is making a comeback."

"Well, there's money in fishing these years," said Brady. "The fishing's been good." More money meant that lobstermen who were so inclined could afford to replace factory-installed engines with bigger ones—adding more horsepower than they needed for carrying traps and gear, but possibly enough to win races. It was customary for fishermen who added power not to admit that they'd done so, but the practice remained among the worst-kept boat racing "secrets."

"It's true," said Olivia. Then she turned with a smile to Mckenna and prodded, "Someday, before ya know it, you'll be out there too."

Mckenna nodded, but didn't quite agree. She wasn't sure if she wanted to try her hand at racing.

"I bet you would, if you had the boat to do it," said Olivia.

"Well," said Mckenna, slowly, as though she were chewing on the possibility, "my turbo was froze up last year, because it had sat for five years before we bought the boat. We were going to find a bigger turbo and put it on there. But Dad said maybe we should wait to put a whole new motor in it, and then we might race it. This year, he took his lobster boat out to race for the first time. It's so big and heavy. It's not designed to race. We went anyway, and we didn't get last. But as soon as we finished he's like, 'Yep, I want a C32 on this thing. I don't want to be last.'"

"When you race," agreed Olivia, "you don't wanna lose. It annoys the living crap out of you. It's competitiveness," she said, nodding to Mckenna, "and you have the same thing."

"Yes, I do," replied Mckenna, with a smile.

"No matter what it is, if it's basketball or if it's racing, or if it's wantin' to throw a ball farther than somebody else," Olivia continued, "then you wanna be able to do it."

"It's always a boy thing though," mused Mckenna. "It's only the men that I get really competitive with."

Olivia laughed. "I know it. I don't like to be told I can't do something, especially by a man. Brady sometimes likes to do it just to aggravate me."

Brady bellowed and leaned back. "I seen this woman a while ago, and we was talking about fishing. So I said to her, 'Girls can't fish.' And she stopped right there, looked at me hard, and said, 'Oh yeah I can, buddy.' And I laughed to think, if she only knew I was married to Olivia—one of the best."

Olivia, who'd made her entry into fishing some twenty-five years earlier than Mckenna, explained what had changed over the years for women in lobstering. "A lot more women are coming up but you gotta know, there's real women that fish, and then there's wannabe women that say they fish just because they want the attention."

Mckenna nodded. "As of right now, just in our area, there's literally me, you, and Isabel, that's running our own boat. That's all."

"There's women who do it that don't live around here," added Olivia, "but I don't know how many of them fish the full eight hundred traps. They might have a couple hundred that they go out and do, which they do themselves. A lot of the others, it's not even their boat. They'll put their oil gear on and take selfies."

Mckenna and Brady laughed. "It's that bad," said Mckenna. "And then you go to, say, a school event. And people say, 'Well this girl fishes, that girl fishes.' And in my head, I'm thinking, 'No they don't.'"

Indeed, recent data show that, despite the undisputed growth of lobstering among Mckenna's generation of girls, less than 5 percent of Maine's commercial lobstering licenses—roughly 200—are held by women. Add in apprenticeship licenses and the number grows by 305; but if previous years' data is any guide, the percentage of those who will go on to become full-time captains will remain low, even while the part-time segment burgeons.

For Olivia and Mckenna, captaining was a badge of honor. The title had been earned with smarts and sweat over a steady progression of seasons. They'd put in the thousand hours of fishing the state required before they could run their own boats—then added plenty more to hone their skills and build a practice marked by steady hauls. Perhaps more than anything, they'd recognized that lobstering wasn't a solo act. Their daily catch was only as good as the sternmen who stood beside them. For Olivia, it was her sister Emily. For Mckenna, it was through a partnership of sorts with her friend Isabel.

The pair worked together through Mckenna's senior year at Narraguagus. Then Mckenna graduated and moved to full-time fishing. Since Isabel was still in school, Mckenna had to turn elsewhere for a regular sternman—most days to her boyfriend Ethan's younger brother. As the season heated up, Mckenna's mom, Phoebe, helped fill in the gaps. Mother and daughter cut a robust image on those waters, living proof that the rough-and-tumble world of Downeast lobster fishing no longer belonged solely to men.

Still, Phoebe wasn't about to trade in her bird's-eye view atop Holt's Wharf for a pair of oil pants. Mckenna would need to find a steady sidekick for the coming season and beyond. Indeed, Mckenna and Isabel might have teamed up like Olivia and Emily, with one as captain and the other as sternman. But both had ambitions that each well understood. Now Isabel—who was heading toward graduation from Narraguagus—was gearing up to captain her own boat full time. "I don't blame her," said Mckenna. "I told her, 'Anytime you need help, I'll go with you.' And she told me, 'Same for you.'"

Chapter 18

Beyond the Sunrise Trail

Josie could still feel the dust on her skin. She could still taste the Mediterranean sea salt that had settled on her lips—mingling the familiar with the exotic. Only a few weeks had passed since she had returned home from her monthlong excursion in Greece—an archaeology dig with an international study program on the island of Antiparos—and her memories of that time were fresh and sweet. Josie had long dreamt of going to Greece. As a child, she'd fallen in love with the Percy Jackson books. Brianna and Dan would take turns reading to the girls, and Josie, being the second youngest, had been exposed early to Jackson's mythological journeys. When she was old enough to read on her own, Josie found herself regularly drawn to Greek myths—and to the Greek art and antiquities that Frannie had introduced in her Narraguagus classroom. Once in Antiparos, Josie had found all that she'd hoped for—and more. She'd been wowed by a female professor who'd led Josie's program at the dig site, and who was part of a well-known husband-and-wife archaeology team. The couple spent much of the year teaching at a Greek university, and summers working on various digs around Greece. Josie dreamt of following in their footsteps.

When she got back from Greece, Josie agreed to help her father with a renovation job he was starting. The old Cherryfield Academy in town was in need of repair now that it had been nearly a decade since its initial restoration. The roof needed fixing, and the windows and trim were due for a new coat of paint. So the academy's trustees had turned to Dan Dekker to freshen up the place. And Josie was poised to help him.

Now, as Josie balanced herself on staging that hugged the old Cherryfield Academy building, she smiled at the thought that she was standing before another relic of sorts. The irony of the academy's architecture didn't escape her either—the grandeur of the two-story Greek Revival structure that had dominated the center of town since the mid-1800s. It was the kind of building that, if you happened to be passing through, you'd stop to admire as quintessentially New England. For nearly a hundred years, until Narraguagus High was built just up the road in Harrington, local high schoolers had gathered here for lessons each day. For a while, the academy building had housed the Cherryfield town hall and library. But by the early 2000s, the once pristine structure had surrendered nearly all of its glory to age and weather. As its oak floors buckled and its heating system sputtered, community members shook their heads and decided something had to be done. The old-timers, who'd been around long enough to remember Cherryfield's better days, began to organize a campaign to restore the old Greek Revival. They were joined in the effort by a new generation of homesteaders, a wave of young parents who'd found their way here from places like New York and New Jersey—in much the same way that Josie's grandparents had some fifty years earlier. These new arrivals were a small but determined group. They were educated—artists, scholars, and musicians peppered their ranks—and as they pondered and created, they also farmed modest organic blueberry fields, homeschooled their children, and gathered fresh eggs from the coops that sat alongside their rustic homes. Old-timers and newcomers banded together to restore the academy building and to refashion it into a community center—a place for fall festivals and weddings, quilt shows and children's story times. This hodgepodge of Cherryfielders had little commonality in their heritage; they rarely saw eye to eye on matters of politics; and their life experiences could not have been more distinct. Yet they broke bread together within the academy's vaunted space and discovered harmony in what they shared.

It was a familiar role for Josie—to stand by Dan's side, paintbrush in hand, ready to help reclaim the dignity of one aging structure or another. In Josie's earlier years, Dan had often taken roofing jobs. Now, his roofing days were almost over. He'd reached an age when climbing atop houses was less than advisable, and Brianna had lovingly, but firmly, counseled him to seek out jobs that would keep his feet more securely planted. And so Dan shifted his energies to designing homes and carpentering, and hired a small crew to help him with construction. The change suited him. In different circumstances, Josie would later reflect, he might have been an architect.

As Dan expanded his scope of work, a stroke of good fortune befell him. Demand for home rehabs and renovations in the area started to accelerate. The spike came not from the locals—most of whom could scarcely afford to pour money into their own dwellings—but from small waves of speculators and summer people who'd seen potential in the old Victorian homes that hugged the Narraguagus River. Buyers from away were scooping up those properties, and cheap, and Dan knew how to transform them. As a result, he'd found himself with more work than he could handle. Six days a week, he'd be out there with his crew, and whichever daughter was available to lend a hand. Whenever Josie joined in the work, she'd admire the changes Dan had helped foster in Cherryfield. She knew it still had a long way to go. But now, when Josie drove through town, she'd remark, "It looks *so* much better than it did ten years ago. There's not junk everywhere."

As Josie scraped and painted another academy windowsill, her mind began to wander. Since she'd arrived home from Greece, her thoughts had often returned to her adventures there. Each time Josie considered the possibilities of what lay ahead, she felt a burst of exhilaration. But every so often, her feelings careened from joy to grief. She knew she had not yet come to terms with the recent death of her uncle Aaron. She'd left home for Greece only a week after she and her family had gathered for his funeral. The escape, reflected Josie, had been exactly what she'd needed. She "was in this new exciting place, loving it, meeting new people, and able to just not think about it."

Uncle Aaron had died unexpectedly, just before Easter, at the age of fifty-one. Josie had been on campus when she'd gotten the call that he had collapsed at his suburban Boston home and been rushed to the hospital. Josie and her family had long known that with Aaron, something like this was possible. He'd struggled for years with health issues, and over time, they'd weakened his heart. His doctor had cautioned him that, if he hoped to see his daughter graduate from high school, he needed to take charge of his destiny—to live healthier and lose weight. So he did. But time was not his ally, and when the ambulance reached the hospital doors, little hope was left.

Josie had come to realize that, in leaving for Greece so soon after the funeral, she'd cut short her process of mourning. Uncle Aaron had always held a piece of her heart, even though he'd long ago moved away from Cherryfield, where he'd grown up beside her mom and her uncle Craig. When Josie was a small child, Grammy Mae and she would often take the bus down to Boston and spend the night at Uncle Aaron's. The memory of those visits had lingered with Josie—the wonder of the Boston Aquarium, the walks along the Freedom Trail, the too-many-to-count occasions that Aaron had surreptitiously slipped Swedish Fish—which Brianna would never allow at home—into Josie's hands. As Josie grew older, Aaron was always there for her and her sisters, and the Dekkers, in turn, were there for Aaron and his wife and daughter. Now, Josie's heart ached for her aunt, and for her cousin, a junior in high school, who was struggling to come to terms with her dad's absence. And Josie began to wonder how a loving God could allow a good man like Aaron to be taken so soon.

When Josie retuned to Yale in the fall, she had not shaken off that question. If anything, it plagued her more. As Josie rediscovered the rhythm of her campus routine, she willed herself to focus on other things. She doubled down on her decision to study art and archaeology. She threw herself into club water polo—and her teammates marveled at how strong an arm she had for someone who'd never played before. Despite her litheness, Josie had always packed power in her limbs. Perhaps it came from all those varsity softball and cross-country seasons at Narraguagus, fortified by years of painting houses and hammering nails on her dad's construction sites. Josie had also eagerly returned to the

Yale Gospel Choir; she'd found fellowship in the group, and in the harmony of the music they made together.

It was, however, the prospect of going back to Bible Study at the YSC, where her sister Angela still worked, that kept nagging at her. She veered back and forth on whether to return, particularly given her state of mind about her faith. In the end, she decided to rejoin, but shied away from the sophomore group that Angela led. Feeling doubt, let alone expressing it, in the face of her big sister, was more than Josie could handle right now.

In Josie's freshman year, she'd gone to church every Sunday at Ridge Street Baptist. "I'd show up there, regardless," she'd say. "Because it was like, it's Sunday, so I go to church." This year, so far, Josie had made it to Ridge Street no more than once or twice a month. The shift hadn't escaped Angela; one day not far into the semester, she'd confronted Josie. The truth was, in addition to the angst that Uncle Aaron's death had prompted, Josie had increasingly felt lost without community—and Ridge Street, although a lovely place to worship, lacked precisely that. After a year of attending services there, Josie couldn't name a member she'd gotten to know. "At home," she mused, "that would never happen." You'd show up once or twice, and "people would come up and they'd hug you." Josie had begun to realize that perhaps, more than anything, it was that sense of community that had kept her tied to church. And at this point, the rest was up for grabs.

Indeed, as fall crept forward, Josie had begun to examine the full sweep of her conservative Independent Baptist upbringing. She still believed in God. But she continued to struggle with why God would allow suffering and untimely death. How was it, she asked, that Uncle Aaron, so kind and loving on earth, might be barred from Heaven? "Yes," she would say, "he went to church when he was growing up in Cherryfield, but I have no idea if he was saved. And if he wasn't, the Bible says, you go to Hell. And I know people have tried to interpret that away. But why would I appreciate this and worship this if that's what happens? Why would you kill someone before they're saved?" Where, she'd begun to wonder, was the evidence that the God of her faith was truly loving?

Josie was bursting with questions—and frustrated that she had neither the time nor the outlet to search for answers. She knew the rules of her church well, but she no longer felt comfortable playing by them. "This is my beef with Christian circles," she reflected. "You're not really allowed to not be okay. The message is 'You're supposed to be a Christian, you're supposed to be uptight and put together.' You're not supposed to talk about things like, 'My friend was really drunk last night and said some disturbing things, and I'm worried about it.' That's not something you would say in a Christian circle." And so Josie began to dig deeper, probing the meaning behind the strictures that had, for so long, shaped her life. She sought insights from her Bible Study leader, and engaged in long discussions with her suitemates.

In time, she came to realize that her disagreements weren't with God, but "with the way people have interpreted the Bible, with the church." And when she—or others like her—raised hard questions, they'd be guided gently back by their teachers to verses, and through those verses, back to interpretations. It was, said Josie, as she threw up her hands, "an endless loop."

Even with her doubts, though, Josie, in her religious practices, stood firmly in the minority among young Americans. A range of surveys have documented weaker religious affiliations among young adults than in previous generations. Today, roughly 30 percent of eighteen-to-twenty-nine-year-olds attend church services at least once a week, and fewer than one fifth attend Bible Study once a week. Still, despite young Americans' low rates of organized participation, they are not, by and large, prepared to abandon faith. More than 70 percent say they're absolutely or fairly certain they believe in God, and two thirds say religion is very or somewhat important in their lives. And although millennials seem to have marched steadily away from structured religiosity as they've come of age, one recent study found signs that trend may be leveling off among Gen Zers, whose ranks Josie and her peers top.

Add rurality to the mix, and overall commitment to religion— even among young adults—intensifies. Small towns across America historically have tended to be more tied to faith and churchgoing than their urban and suburban counterparts. A nearly twenty-year-old Gallup study documented the longtime gap, and found that the older average age of rural residents only in part accounted for differences. More recently, University of New Hampshire researchers found that a majority of rural Americans across all ages who live in "declining resource" or chronically poor communities attend church at least once a week, compared with less than a third in similarly sparse "amenity rich" areas. Assessing the mix of data, there's no question that a push and pull exists around questions of faith and organized prayer among America's young, and that the inner conflicts Josie faced were far from uncommon.

As the semester wore on, Josie responded to those conflicts by stepping back from her Bible Study group. She needed space to figure things out, "without the influence of all these people who are so confident, in theory, in what they believe. Because the thing is," she'd say quietly, "they're probably not." She turned her focus increasingly to the gospel choir. She saw it as a bridge, a nondenominational faith group that was "looser on theology" than Bible Study, that embraced Christians and non-Christians alike. And she found in it a space that said "bring your questions and your mess and we'll sift through it. Because we're all there too."

She also began to test the waters of her doubt with her mom. One day, Josie turned to Brianna and said, "I don't agree with what our church preaches." She'd continued to struggle over verses, particularly those that placed women in a submissive role. Her entire life, the church had dictated an onslaught of rules. Dress conservatively. Don't show your shoulders. Wait for a Christian young man. Reach high, but do not surpass your husband in your goals.

It hadn't always been that way at the Harrington church in which Josie had been raised. In her early years, the pastor had preached "from a place of love," and had created a haven for prayer and reflection that Josie and her family had found uplifting. In that time, the Dekkers had grown close to the pastor and his family. The pastor's daughter, Chloe, had remained Josie's best friend even after the girls' Bumble Bee Club trio, which included Vivian, had been disbanded. When Josie was in third grade, the pastor and his family had moved. With their departure, the community found itself without a spiritual leader. It would take more than two years for Lighthouse Baptist to get a new pastor; through that period, the church members rallied to minister themselves. Brianna played piano for services, and Dan played the guitar. They gathered and worshipped, strengthened by their love of God, their connection to one another, and the praise music that lifted their hearts. In Josie's ninth-grade year, yet another pastor arrived. He and his wife also ministered from a place of love, but combined their teachings with a firm hand. They told Josie's dad they no longer wanted him to play the guitar at services. There was, they said, no place for praise music in the church.

Once, after Josie had returned from her ninth-grade mission trip to the Dominican Republic, she'd told the pastor's wife—who was also her Sunday school teacher—that she'd like to explore the idea of missionary work. Josie had been attracted by the adventure of it, the chance to travel *and* talk to people about God. In response, "the pastor's wife said, 'I'll pray that your husband's a missionary.'" The following year, after Josie's second missionary trip, she'd set her sights on becoming a surgeon. She'd been inspired by what she'd learned about the work of Doctors Without Borders. She'd talked about the possibility excitedly, and again her teacher had met her with rebuke. Indeed, Sunday school was peppered with lessons that Josie rejected. Female pastors were verboten. God called men to do different jobs than women. Both within and beyond the household, men should lead and women should serve.

These were not the lessons Josie had learned in her own home. Brianna and Dan had navigated their life together arm in arm, as equals. And they had vowed to each other, *we will not raise our daughters any different than we would a son.* As the four girls grew and talk would turn to boys and dating—as well as to their academic and professional pursuits—Brianna would tell them never to accept a secondary status. Looking down the line, she'd say, "Your marriage needs to be a partnership, or else it's never going to work."

Josie knew there was a softly whispered divide within the church. There were, on the one hand, the leaders in thought—those members who were strong in their faith *and* secure in how they lived their lives, no matter who stood at the pulpit or what they preached. Those members, said Josie, would basically say, "Pastors come and go. Sometimes they're wack, sometimes they're legit. But I know my beliefs and I'm gonna follow them." And then there were members for whom "whatever the pastor said was right." There was little room to reconcile the two—and no in-house perch from which to challenge the church's authority.

Josie also knew that her parents were firmly planted in the first group. In recent years, Brianna and Dan had toyed with the idea of finding another church. For Brianna, said Josie, "It came down to one of two things: Do I want a church that preaches more of what I believe, or do I stay here because this is where my church family is?" It wasn't an easy call, but in the end, Brianna and Dan decided it was more important to remain with their community. The Dekkers had invested a good deal in Lighthouse Baptist. They'd spent eighteen years as a family there. Josie's mom had grown up in those pews. Pappy Stuart and Dan had been deacons there for as long as Josie could remember. The ladies who'd watched over Brianna when she was a little girl now looked upon all four Dekker girls as though they were their own grandchildren. And Josie's own Grammy Mae had been the church treasurer for years. Indeed, for Brianna and Dan—and for Josie too—the sum of Lighthouse Baptist's parts was irreplaceable. It was "forever."

Now, as Josie waded further into the realm of big questions with her mom, she considered the magnitude of where they both were headed. She and Brianna had always been close, but they'd never really touched on "the uncomfortable." At first, their talks were a bit rocky. Josie often felt she had to prepare Brianna for where she'd wanted to lead the conversations. It was around this time that Josie told Brianna "some things that happened" when she was in middle school in Cherryfield—things that she now understood would be considered sexual assault, even though no one back then had acknowledged they'd even occurred. For instance, Josie had told her mom, that "you can't just go grab a girl's butt."

Brianna had turned to Josie and said, "Wait. That's still happening? Why wouldn't you have told me in seventh grade that people were grabbing your butt?"

"I couldn't," said Josie, "I'd have been too embarrassed."

"That happened to me in school," Brianna responded, shaken by her daughter's disclosure. "But that was in the seventies."

And so Josie began to tell her mom things she never before would have, things "that needed to change"—not just in her hometown, but in other places. Indeed, Josie and her friends had encountered harassment while in Greece—from certain men on the dig site, at restaurants, or simply walking down the street. At times, it was so pervasive that one of the guys in Josie's group had taken on the role of pretending to be her boyfriend, just to keep the most persistent men at bay. Josie, too, had learned to assert herself, both in Greece and when out with friends at Yale. And if a guy got too friendly too fast, she'd have no problem making her message clear.

As Josie continued to question and discover, to open doors of inquiry and memory with her mom, she did not recoil from the community in which she'd grown up—the community she knew she would someday leave behind forever. Indeed, she continued to embrace her time at home. At each semester's end, she would leave school as soon as she could, and at each break's close, she'd return to campus as late as possible. "I guess," she'd say, "I do that because Yale is where I spend most of my time. I feel like it's okay if I wait two more days to see these people, because I'm about to see them for a whole semester."

And although Josie had made plenty of friends in her first year and a half at Yale, she did not march in lockstep with the vast majority of students there. "I'm fairly liberal," she would say, "for most of the world"—and certainly for Downeast Maine—"but at Yale I am a moderate." Josie and her suitemates, who had been matched to live together as freshmen, often bonded over where they stood among their college peers. "We are not conservative people, but Yale is *so* liberal." Indeed, Josie had participated in protests on and around campus—she'd marched in support of sexual assault victims and against Brett Kavanaugh's Supreme Court appointment. She'd participated in a walkout to demand Yale's divestment from fossil fuel companies, and had taken to the football field with climate-change activists at the Harvard-Yale game. But she was not comfortable demonizing those who came to the table with opposing points of view. When it came to staking out political ground, said Josie, "I feel like we need something in the middle. We need to get rid of the polarization first in order to get something done. I reject the idea that 'all Republicans are evil.' I grew up in an area with a lot of nice Republicans. They're not evil. They just have different ideas. We need to be able to work with both sides."

Chapter 19

Something Better

Winter came early Downeast, much as it always does, and with the frost came the inevitable drumbeat of change in Willow's life.

Willow had been trying to make her long-distance relationship with Robert work. But with summer came her busy work season at the wharf, and the days of opportunity to visit him quickly began to slip away. She never did make it out to Michigan, and as summer moved into full swing, Willow began to feel more distance from him. Finally, in July, she told him, *I can't do everything and not feel bad about not being able to talk to you and spend time with you.* And as evenly as they had rekindled their relationship, they ended it.

And then she met Jethro. Who was twenty-five and charming, and a born-and-bred Downeaster. The pair met on Facebook, after Jethro friended Willow from the "People You May Know" list. He was a fisherman—a sternman on a local lobster boat. He'd found his way onto one vessel or another since he was fourteen, and in that time, he'd worked hard and earned good money doing it.

It didn't take long for Willow and Jethro to realize that they'd previously been "intertwined in each other's lives." Some time back, their dads had worked together on a boat. When Willow's dad learned that she'd started dating Jethro, he was furious. At the time, Willow hadn't yet told her mom about Jethro, but William beat her to the punch. He called Lily and said that Willow was making the biggest mistake of her life because she "was getting involved with the wrong boy." From this, Willow would learn that her dad thought Jethro was "mean and arrogant," and worst of all, that William had heard "rumors that Jethro had beat on women before." True, William's objections betrayed a stunning lack of self-reflection. But he persisted, so much so that Willow finally confronted Jethro with the rumors. Jethro denied them, and something in Willow's instinct told her to trust that his words were true.

It was also in July that Willow found herself in the midst of another of Dad's rage storms. This time, the target of his anger was his longtime girlfriend, Maria. It was early evening, and Willow and her brothers all happened to be at Dad's house. Maria had been out drinking, lost track of time, and arrived home two hours late. Willow was upstairs in her room, packing some things to spend another night with Jethro. Even from there, she could feel Dad's anger building. Dad didn't like it when someone wasn't home when they said they'd be.

From the moment Maria walked through the door, the yelling began, and all Willow could think was *how do I get the boys out?* The last time Willow had seen her dad that pissed, he'd hurt Mom. As the fight unfolded, Scott and Isaac were "going up and down the stairs." Willow was worried that "one of them might get in the way, or say the wrong thing when Dad was in that mindset." She grabbed them and told them to get their stuff together, and "messaged Mom about taking the boys to her house, but she wasn't home." Then she texted Jethro and asked for his help. Willow hadn't yet told Jethro about her past, and now the "family secret" that had plagued Willow all her life was about to unfold before his eyes. She wrote, *I'm sorry to ask you this but I don't feel safe at my dad's right now. Can I please go to your house?* And he said, *Yes, of course you can.* But mostly, "he was so upset at the idea that my dad may have hit one of us kids, or had in the past."

From that night on, Willow spent most of her time at Jethro's; she hadn't officially moved in with him, but she barely saw her dad, and only returned to his house to pick up what she needed and check her mail. Meanwhile, William had tired of waiting for state regulators to begin granting recreational marijuana licenses and had abandoned hopes of opening his own pot shop. Instead, he'd taken a job at a medical marijuana dispensary in Machias, but after a while he'd walked away from that too. Now he was "doing wood carvings in the basement and selling them." He was mostly carving "names of people's boats in the area." It wasn't clear how long his latest venture might last, but for the moment, he was intent on making a go of it. In September, William messaged Willow and gave her an ultimatum: "Move back in" with him, or get the rest of her stuff and take it to Jethro's. He told her he needed to know because he didn't have enough money to heat his basement, and wanted to convert her upstairs bedroom into his wood-carving shop.

Willow and Jethro talked about living together full time, even though they'd barely been together for two months. But it felt good, and natural, to Willow. Her anxiety and depression, which had clung to her when she'd lived with Lee, had melted away. Indeed, life was "nothing like it was with Lee—crying all the time and always being worried." With Jethro, Willow was "happy, content, and just living." And Jethro was kind, and shared in the responsibilities of life with her. She collected what was left of her belongings from Dad's, and hoped that this might be the move that marked the end of her nomadic life.

Meanwhile, as Willow's relationship soared, her dad's fell to pieces. In October, William and Maria split up. Maria's drinking, said Willow, "had gotten a lot worse, and Dad, who was still sober, had finally had enough." Willow had since recovered from the summer incident at the house, but after she moved out for good, she barely talked to William. It had been a long time since Willow had seen her dad explode, and with Jethro by her side, she felt safer than she'd ever felt before, and more secure in her own strength.

As this, the autumn of Willow's contentment, waned, she felt a surge of optimism. Her work at the wharf had slowed as, once again, the fishermen began to scrub their lobster boats and pull them in for winter's dormancy. She took advantage of the quiet around her, hunkered down with her schoolwork, and braced herself for her midterm push. Willow had found her coursework to be tougher than it had been the previous year, but she didn't mind the challenge. Indeed, she welcomed it. And even though the scholarship money she'd gotten her freshman year had run dry, financial aid alone continued to carry the load for her. Once again she came out ahead, getting more than a thousand dollars beyond what she needed for school. Between that and the money she earned and saved from her work at the wharf—not to mention Jethro's steady pay—Willow could honestly say that life, for her, had never been better.

Just after Christmas, Jethro asked Willow to marry him. At that stage, it was more of a promise than a plan, but the ring was on Willow's finger nonetheless, and the aura of something permanent had wrapped itself around her heart. Willow knew that she and Jethro would have to hold off on a wedding until he was able to pay off the back debt he owed, but she was also certain it was only a temporary hurdle. And although Willow dreamed of starting a family, the pair had agreed to wait at least until Willow finished college—and until Jethro's three-year-old daughter, Joyce, turned five.

Vivian initially learned of Willow's news from a Facebook post on the night of the engagement. The next day, Willow texted Vivian with the bombshell. Vivian wasn't upset, or surprised, that Willow had spread the word to her virtual world before sharing the news with her best friend. Deep down, Vivian figured, Willow must have known that Vivian might warn her not to jump into something big so quickly again.

In truth, Vivian was happy for Willow. She'd met Jethro in August, not long after he and Willow had started to date, and had liked him. Most of all, she'd liked that he seemed to be nothing like Lee. And even though Vivian would remain protective of Willow, she knew enough to keep her layers of feelings in check—because "if something were to happen," and Willow and Jethro's relationship were to fall apart, Vivian wanted Willow to know that she could turn to her. She "didn't want Willow not to have anybody."

Three weeks after the engagement, Willow sent Vivian another text, this one more jarring than the first. In it, Willow confided that she was pregnant. The news stopped Vivian's heart. When Willow later revealed that she was joking, Vivian wasn't entirely surprised. Sometimes Willow would lob a shocker Vivian's way to test the waters. Vivian knew Willow had long wanted a child of her own. Indeed, she recognized the lure it held for Willow, whose grasp had slipped, too many times to count, from the rungs of unconditional love. Still, Vivian knew that the timing would be wrong for Willow, that having a child before she finished school would likely derail her life. Too many girls she'd grown up with had gone that route, and Vivian wanted more for her friend.

Whether or not they attend college, girls Downeast overwhelmingly marry, and have children, young. According to a 2016 study conducted by economist Caitlin Myers for *The New York Times*, the average age of first-time mothers in Washington County is 24.1. That's nearly five years younger than the average age in Maine's Portland area, and well below the national average of 26.3. The average first-time motherhood age in Washington County for women without a college degree, as well as for unmarried women, hovers around 23.

Indeed, whatever their age, Downeasters who decide to marry before having a child find themselves in a minority among women in their county. In 2018, unwed mothers accounted for 53 percent of Washington County's births, nearly 20 points above both Maine's and the nation's average. That number puts Washington County within one point of Mississippi, the state with the highest percentage of births to unmarried mothers.

It's important to note that for some in Maine and elsewhere across America—and particularly for those with means (who tend to be older, have college degrees, and have established careers)—single motherhood increasingly represents a choice that comes with rich experiences and opportunities, and a strong support network for children. But the vast majority of single-parent households have insufficient income to meet their kids' needs. According to the Children's Defense Fund, in 2016 the poverty rate for children who lived in single-parent households was more than four times that of kids growing up in married-couple families. A significant body of research has also documented that children who grow up in low-income single-parent households are less likely to complete school, more likely to earn lower incomes as young adults, and more likely to be in poverty themselves by age twenty-five than children of married adults.

Willow didn't need statistical data to recognize that despite her eagerness for a child of her own, she would be better off doing so with Jethro by her side. She felt fortunate to have a partner with whom she could build a future and support a family. At the same time, she couldn't shake her disappointment in the latest unraveling of her relationship with her dad, whom she hadn't seen or spoken with in months. He messaged her occasionally to alert her that some of her mail was sitting at his place, and he'd sent a text acknowledging her engagement. But beyond that, silence. Willow tried to keep up with news about him through her brother Scott, who still lived with him. She was relieved to know that William remained sober, although she sensed that Maria might be back in the picture. The status of their relationship on any given day, said Willow, was "kind of whatever Dad feels like telling people at the moment." Meanwhile, Willow's mom, Lily, was making her way through nursing school, while continuing to raise Willow's youngest brother, Isaac. Despite the hurdles Lily had encountered along the way, she was determined to finish her degree. She'd been accepted as a transfer student to the University of Maine Augusta's program, whose Ellsworth campus wasn't far from the hospital in which she worked as a nurse's aide. Willow figured the school transfer was bound to make Lily's life a little easier. At least, that's what she hoped.

In February, Willow thought she might be pregnant—this time for real. Excited as she was, and even though she knew she and Jethro were solid, she suddenly felt unready. She wondered how she would juggle motherhood with work, school, two dogs, and the responsibility of helping care for Joyce twice a week. It wasn't that Willow minded any of it. She loved looking after Joyce, and had developed a strong bond with her in a short time—even as she jokingly complained that the toddler had "missed the terrible twos and moved right into the threatening threes." It was, in Willow's view, an added bonus that Joyce's mom lived only a few minutes away. Willow texted regularly with her to manage pickups and drop-offs, and the two "got along just fine."

In the end, Willow's pregnancy fears were for naught. There was, the doctor said, a ruptured cyst—a casualty of a chronic condition, polycystic ovary syndrome, that Willow had lived with for years. It had been a while since something like this had happened to her, but the ordeal was a stark reminder that pregnancy, for Willow, along with roughly five million American women who shared the condition, brought risk. For now, though, Willow set those realities aside and breathed a sigh of relief.

Winter marched on. After a monthlong stint on a scallop boat in Massachusetts, Jethro had found steady scalloping work out of a local wharf—and come spring, he'd again take up the job of sternman on a nearby lobster boat. Each morning, he would awaken at 4:00 a.m., and Willow would rise with him. In the predawn hours, as he headed out to fish, she'd make her way to her desk at the wharf, well before she was expected. She treasured the silence of those hours and found, amid the clutter, her most productive school and work time.

By mid- to late afternoon, Willow and Jethro would routinely return home, and the pair would unwind together. Since meeting Jethro, Willow had started smoking pot as a way to relax. At first, she'd hesitated. She'd seen what drug use had done to her dad. Willow knew he'd begun smoking pot when he was twelve—and as his years of use progressed and mingled with more insidious drugs, Willow and her brothers had become unwitting casualties of "the way it controlled him and his life." She would watch her dad and think, "I don't want to have to crave something as bad as you crave it, to have to hit your children or your wife because you have to spend money on them instead of going to get drugs."

It was in those early years that Willow had vowed never to experiment with drugs. Once she'd turned eighteen, she had given it a brief go, but soon decided it wasn't for her. "Then, after Jethro, I tried it again. I got used to it, and realized there's different types of weed." Now, Willow smoked whenever the mood struck. "Sometimes," she reflected, "with my anxiety the way it is, it really helps. Especially if I've had a bad day."

All in all, Willow and Jethro had found themselves in a contented place, and they began to allow themselves to dream of something better. *What if,* they'd say to each other, *what if we could figure out a way to start our own business?* They talked about selling seafood. "If we opened up something," Willow imagined, "I could use my business degree, and we could be our own bosses. Make our own hours. And spend more time with Joyce. Jethro could go out on the boat and get seafood, and we could have a shop, or a truck, and take it to people and deliver it places."

They talked, too, about picking up and moving elsewhere in Maine, not to an urban hotspot like Portland, or a major hub like Augusta or Bangor. The life those places offered was too fast, too crowded, and unsettlingly unfamiliar. Rather, their dream was to wander farther off the grid, perhaps north and west to Greenville, which sits on the edge of the state's iconic Moosehead Lake and holds the honor of being the best place for moose watching in all of Maine. When Willow got to talking about the possibility, her unflappable Downeast tone gained an uncharacteristic lilt. These past few months, she had begun to allow herself to feel more hope than ever before—and she'd gained strength from the unfolding of it. True, Willow had always been adaptable to change. Perhaps that adaptability came from all the bouncing around she'd done as a child. Perhaps it came from recognizing that certainty was a luxury reserved for girls more fortunate than her. Whatever the reason, one thing was sure: never before had change felt so liberating.

It was that sense of freedom that allowed Willow to reawaken old passions, starting with her love of photography. Now, as in her high school days, she began to carry her camera with her. Her photos, always well executed, took on a newfound texture. Today, her work was portraiture of a higher order. It was populated with, and defined by, Willow's three loves—Jethro, Joyce, and the inexhaustible majesty of the Downeast sea. Indeed, it was the sea that moved her most of all, as it always had. "I'm in love with it," she would say, "I love the idea that it's so free that no one can control it. It controls everyone else, because one tsunami and we're done for, one hurricane and we're flooded, one wrong move and the boat is sunk." But that, said Willow, is "the ultimate thing"—to see and experience the power of the ocean, to know it would always be there, steps away. In those moments, Willow knew that she "would never leave such a beautiful place," and that it would fall on her generation to "make it better."

Indeed, through her relationship with Jethro, Willow discovered new ways to expand her embrace of the sea and the land that it surrounded. She began to ice fish and to hunt. Willow found herself suited to the feel of the gun in her hand, and the rush of standing beside Jethro as he hit a stag. For as long as she could remember, she'd wanted to learn to hunt. Growing up, she'd watched most of the kids around her go off for Hunting Days with their families. None of the adults around her was willing to take the time to teach her, so she never got the chance. Hunting with Jethro represented yet another rectification of the casualties of her childhood.

As Willow sat in the stillness of Jethro's house—the house she now called her own—she daydreamed about the life the pair might have if they could only pull together enough for that spot off Moosehead Lake. She'd thought of the time they'd spend fishing and hunting, the way the light of the sun would frolic atop the wide stretch of liquid calm, and the possibility of capturing on camera the faint silhouette of a mother shepherding her calf across the banks of the verdant shore. Still, though the harmony of it beckoned her, she knew she would never fully abandon her Downeast life. Despite the childhood and adolescent nightmares fomented in it, it was her home. "I'm tied to this place," she'd say, her eyes as placid as dewdrops, "and I always will be."

Willow is hardly alone among rural Americans in her attachment to the place in which she was born and raised. A 2018 Pew Research Center survey found that rural residents are more likely to want to stay in their communities than their urban and suburban counterparts. They are also more likely to live near extended family, and know all or most of their neighbors. And contrary to popularized notions of a "brain drain," one recent study discovered that top-achieving rural students have "the highest community attachment" of their peers—indeed, among youth across all achievement levels who do leave, top achievers are those most likely to want to return. Their attachment is fostered by "the close-knit nature of the community and school environment," the personal attention and opportunities that come with being in a small school, and an overall "sense of belonging and inclusiveness."

This is not to say that concerns don't exist. Worries about job availability are higher in rural areas than in cities and suburbs, and average earnings per worker are lowest (even after accounting for cost-of-living differences). And overall employment among "prime-age workers" in rural areas declined from 2000 to 2018, while rising in cities and suburbs. Linked to this phenomenon are the challenges of internet access and transportation, which are significantly larger rural concerns.

But something different seems to be occurring now: people are coming to, and staying in, rural America.

Along a central hallway of Narraguagus High, there is a poster with the words: "Staying isn't Settling." It's surrounded by photos of alums who have distinguished themselves beyond their high school careers—particularly those who've decided to remain or return to the area. Evidence, both statistical and anecdotal, indicates that in this and other parts of rural America, the message that staying is not settling can hold strong sway. The strength of emotional, familial, and community-oriented ties is significant, and may ultimately be proving determinative in the choices rural youth make to commit to, and ultimately improve, their hometowns—even while economic opportunities lag and the burdens of distances to key services persist.

Chapter 20

Regaining Faith

Vivian sat in the camper and sighed. Hours earlier, she'd been sent home by her boss at Saldon House, a Houlton-based nursing home and residential care facility. Vivian had been working longer shifts at Saldon, and more of them, since COVID-19 had cast its shadow on the nation. Now it was nearly April, and her schedule showed no sign of letting up. In the previous week alone, she'd logged eighty hours.

It wasn't that Vivian minded working. She'd been raised on work, and plenty of it. In the year she'd been studying in Fort Kent and working at Saldon, she never once called in sick. She'd taken her rolling shifts without complaint—day into evening, evening into night, and over again. But residential care wasn't the type of nursing work she'd dreamed of; she'd rather be training in the ER, or on a frantic hospital floor. She'd rather be doing more.

Still, Vivian was grateful for the experience. The money helped too. She and Andy were saving what they could toward a house of their own. They knew their goal was years, not months, away, but she felt no pressure to move out of Andy's parents' house. She called them her family. And they were. Of course she loved her parents. She worried about her stepmom, who was battling breast cancer, and her grandparents, whose bodies were wearing down. She even, at times, looked back fondly on slivers of her Downeast life. But the intimacy of Vivian's hometown still stifled, the scars from her adolescent struggles still lingered, and the community's culture of watchfulness still suffocated. Perhaps someday those feelings would fade.

The irony was that Houlton, to an outsider's eyes, was not so different from Harrington. It was bigger, to be sure, but with fewer than six thousand people, it was hardly a metropolis. It wasn't a wealthy place; median incomes were not much higher than those Downeast. True, Houlton had more amenities, more restaurants, bars, and stores within reach. But it was colder, snowier, and despite being more densely populated, geographically more remote than Harrington. Pushed up against the Canadian border, in the vast northeastern county of Aroostook, Houlton, like Harrington, took its code of self-sufficiency seriously.

Indeed, in ways familiar to Vivian, Houlton was a community of small-town sensibilities, a place where locals' histories and destinies were interlaced. It was also a town where family names carried weight, not for the status of their job titles, but for the centrality and longevity of their generations, and for all they'd contributed, in toil and perseverance, to making Houlton what it was today. The distinction, for Vivian, was that Houlton was not "of the Westfords." It didn't require of her what Harrington required; it didn't ask her to be anything other than what she wanted to be.

So it was that in trading one enclave for another, Vivian had found her place. In Houlton, she was surrounded by the Carsons, who, not unlike the Westfords, bore a proud local reputation. She was sheltered by a populace that welcomed her as an extension of the Carsons' embrace of her. And perhaps for the first time in her young life, Vivian felt truly happy.

Then came COVID-19. Or at least, in the most rural parts of Maine, the anticipation of it. Even in the far reaches of Houlton, government leaders' fears of viral spread upended daily life and threatened to shatter the communal foundation that distinguished small-town life. To some, it seemed unlikely that the virus could find its way to the realm of the preternaturally socially distanced. But little was known and understood about the disease and few were willing to take risks. This was especially true with vulnerable populations in places like Harrington and Houlton—whose median age, bevy of high-risk conditions, and limited access to health care represented three strikes against them. Uncertainty bred caution, and isolated communities heeded orders to isolate even more.

As Vivian huddled in the narrow camper, she took comfort in knowing that the odds of a positive test result for the Saldon resident she'd cared for were low. Still, her mind raced. *If it's positive and I've contracted it,* she thought to herself, *I'm at peace with that. I'm young, and strong enough. But if I've exposed Andy's parents, I don't know what I'll do.* Andy's dad was a diabetic. His mom had a chronic autoimmune disease. She knew that, for them, severe consequences—perhaps even death—could follow.

Vivian was tired. Every muscle, bone, and joint in her body ached. All she wanted to do was hug Andy and crawl into bed. Instead she was quarantined, like millions of Americans who suspected they might have been exposed to the virus.

When the word came that the Saldon resident had tested

negative, Vivian felt a surge of relief. Then she called her boss and gave notice. She felt certain she had to quit the job. But in her heart she remained conflicted. Vivian was never one to abandon a challenge. She knew that by choosing to study nursing she'd willingly embraced the call to take risks and make sacrifices in service to others. She felt guilty for stepping back while so many around her were stepping up. She'd explored volunteering for what had been informally dubbed Maine's "pandemic team"—an effort to corral the state's medical personnel for the possibility of a major COVID-19 onslaught. The call had been extended to nursing students who were two or more years into their programs. But Vivian had been counseled that her arthritis could put her at greater risk should she contract the virus. She also knew that if she were to be deployed, she'd have to move out of the Carsons' house, at least temporarily, and separate herself from Andy and his family. It was, to Vivian, too high a price to pay, financially and emotionally. And yet, Vivian was torn. "I feel like I shouldn't be backing away from this, because I could be doing my part. But I'm still human. I don't have that much medical experience. I have family members that could be put at risk. It's so hard . . . because I know nursing is what I want to do with my life. I've prayed about it a lot, and I honestly don't know what the right answer is."

Indeed, in this, the spring of COVID-19, Vivian had found herself praying more. For so long she'd felt frustrated, burdened really, by her church back home in Harrington. She had abandoned what she'd grown up with, and left it to wither, until there was almost nothing left of it inside her.

But nursing school—and perhaps, she recognized, the wisdom that comes with having grown a little older—had nudged her to a different place. "It's not to say I'm giving up on questioning things," she said, "but being able to pick something, to believe that God is real and that He's there in some form, it's become more grounding for me."

When she was being honest with herself, Vivian gave her parents credit for knowing this moment would come, for knowing her, in some ways, better than she knew herself. "They both told me this would happen," she conceded. "That eventually I'd get to the point where I'd feel better about deciding. And I do. The truth is, it's always been in times of crisis in my life that I've had a big restoration of faith. I wouldn't say that I'm a Christian, or that I'm something else, specifically. I don't know how I feel about all that other stuff, the organization of it, the rules. But I do believe in my heart that there's a God."

Vivian paused, as if to take in her acknowledgment. "I need that belief to keep me going. And I've found that people around me in the medical field, a lot of them need it too. Because so much of what the medical world is, is dying. A lot more than you think there is, until you get into it."

So it was that, as Vivian watched COVID-19 wreak havoc across the globe and considered the possibility that it could land in her protected sphere, she re-embraced her faith. "I'm not freakishly religious," she reflected. "But I think we're in bad times. We have more hate and discontent than we've seen among people in a long time. And now we have this illness." Vivian stopped and drew a sharp breath. "I'm not one of those people who says, 'It's the end of the world.' But it does make me question, 'Have we done this? Have we brought this on in some way?' Treating our world like garbage. Behaving terribly. It makes you ask a lot of questions, whether you're religious or not. And everybody, no matter what they believe, is asking, 'Why did this happen? Why?'"

A week after Vivian had quit Saldon House, she reversed course. The nursing home management had offered to put her up in a cabin nearby, owned by one of the staff nurses, while she worked. Vivian gladly took the offer, and felt a sense of peace that, however things unfolded with this virus in her corner of the world, she'd not be standing idly by.

Chapter 21

Fighting Back

As it turned out, COVID-19 was slow to spread to rural America—and although it eventually came, for the most part it did so in drips, not waves. The first case in a rural county was not reported until late February, a full month after health officials had marked the virus's entry into the United States, and it wasn't until mid-March that Maine saw its first COVID patients. By the time Vivian had decided to return to Saldon House, Maine's confirmed case count barely topped five hundred.

It would, in those months, not be the virus, so much as the cascade of secondary economic effects, that would set places like Downeast Washington County back on their heels. The trouble Downeast began in January, with a sudden freefall in wholesale demand for lobsters—a massive supply-chain disruption that landed at Maine's doorstep. First, cargo planes in Canada, a major lobster seller to China, sharply cut back on flights to Asia when the Chinese government responded to COVID-19 with a countrywide lockdown. Then, the resultant oversupply of Canadian lobsters spilled over to the States, driving Maine lobster prices precipitously downward. Soon after, as stay-at-home orders blanketed the nation, restaurants began to close—eliminating the source of nearly 70 percent of the country's seafood consumption for roughly two months. With no market for their lobsters, Maine's commercial fishing industry took a huge gut punch and went down for the count. Vessels sat idle, wharf-based and fish-processing workers were laid off, and lobster pounds and other seafood wholesalers shuttered their doors. Downeast, fishermen started to do the math in their head, and it wasn't pretty. In Washington County alone, losing a lobstering season would amount to an eighty-million-dollar hit. Factor in clams, elvers, and other assorted catches, and the reach would extend to huge swaths of the area's households.

The only silver lining was that the shutdowns began in late winter and early spring, before many of the small-vessel lobstermen got started for the year. The March shutdowns affected primarily larger boats, which were sturdy enough to brave weather conditions throughout the year, and whose captains had been able to set their traps in federal waters three miles or more offshore. More compact craft, like Mckenna's and Olivia Marshall's, typically sat idle longer into the spring—and only kicked into full gear with the approach of summer. Perhaps, if the shutdowns were lifted by May or June, there would still be time for them to salvage some of lobstering's high season.

As Downeast fishermen braced themselves for possible calamity, workers in other sectors across Maine were already in freefall. By early May, nearly one in five Maine workers had filed for unemployment. It was a brutal statistic, but the real concern was for what lay ahead. A lost summer would extend well beyond Maine's fisheries. It would spell disaster for the state's tourism business—a six-billion-dollar industry that generated more than 16 percent of the state's jobs. One study, conducted by Oxford Economics, named Maine as "the most economically vulnerable" state in the nation as a result of COVID-19. The state's "elderly populations, dependence on retail activity, and the prevalence of small business" combined for a potentially crippling mix.

For Downeast Washington County residents in particular, the possibility of long-term harm was terrifying. Their region had been among the last to climb out of the hole dug by the Great Recession of 2008. For most of the decade that followed, Washington County held the unfortunate distinction of maintaining the highest unemployment rate of Maine's sixteen counties. By the start of 2020, despite a roaring national economy, many Downeast families—particularly those not fortunate enough to own lobster boats—were still recovering. Another blow could prove devastating.

Staring out at Pleasant Bay from her home, Mckenna Holt took the news of Maine's downturn with trademark reticence. A few months earlier, she'd been celebrating her best lobstering year ever. Now, the entire fishing season was in jeopardy. It wasn't just her own fishing prospects that worried Mckenna. The future of Holt's Wharf, to which the entire family's fate was tied, hung in the balance.

True, the Holts were a prudent lot. They'd built their business conservatively, and had managed to keep a reserve should times turn bad. But COVID-19 had packed a wallop beyond anyone's imagination. "Before all this happened," said Mckenna, "I was planning on fishing a lot more this year, because I wasn't planning to play soccer again in the fall, and the only day I would be down to the college would be Mondays." With two or three more days a week in the water, she might have doubled what she'd made the previous year. Now she wasn't sure if she'd be able to fish at all.

For lobstering families here—the Holts, the Bartons, and the Marshalls—the gains of lobstering's good years, and indeed, the future of Maine's lobster industry, were in peril. And no one in these parts, not even the Holts, could afford to lose an entire fishing season.

As spring approached, Olivia Marshall took stock of what she and her husband, Brady, and so many fishermen like them, faced. The price of lobster had "dropped to almost half what it should be for this time of year." Brady, who, unlike Olivia, lobstered year-round, felt the shutdown's effects almost immediately. The pound Brady regularly sold to "wasn't buying," so he and Olivia had resorted to selling lobsters to locals from home. "The price wasn't good," said Olivia, "but at least he was able to sell what little he caught." No one needed to remind Olivia how significant it was to have neighbors looking out for each other. Indeed, what kept the Marshalls, and other local lobstermen, going was that "our community has been so good, trying to support the local fishermen. They don't have much, but they've helped us get the word out. They've bought lobster, clams, and other local seafood from us—probably more than they needed, just to be of help."

Meanwhile, Olivia made plans to delay her spring fishing schedule. Typically, like most inshore fishermen, she'd begin setting her gear by end of May. Now, in the best-case scenario, she'd start in late June. "With the catch of so little product," she lamented, "combined with the low price of lobsters, you can hardly afford the cost to even unhook your boat." No matter how sparse demand might be, Olivia still had to ante up for the usual expenses: "Fuel, bait, paying for your sternmen, insurance, and boat payments. It's not practical."

And of course, said Olivia, that wasn't the whole story. "Fishermen here aren't the only ones struggling. There are so many local businesses and restaurants that have had to close because of the virus, and that's not only a huge hit to them, but to the whole community. People are doing the best they can to keep others safe. If anyone needs anything, there are really great people that will step up and do what they can." Still, Olivia acknowledged, it was anyone's guess where things might end up for the community she loved. "It's a scary situation for all of us. We all have fears and concerns about our safety and economic survival. We can only do our part and take it one day at a time, and pray that we all can bounce back from this."

Craig Palmer sat in his office and looked to more than prayer for answers. The Downeast native, and uncle of Josie Dekker, had never seen such dire prospects for the lobster industry—or for the broader community. Since the state-imposed quarantine, he'd taken to stopping occasionally at his workplace, the only economic development hub in Washington County. More often, he was up at his parents' beef and dairy farm—Grammy Mae and Pappy Stuart's place—for which he now shepherded much of the day-to-day business. Meanwhile, his husband, Brayden, who ran and co-owned a Harrington-based bakery with Craig, scrambled to keep up with a surge in wholesale demand for bread. Craig and Brayden were fortunate. Maine's stay-at-home order had brought an uptick in business at the farm and bakery. Late-winter sales suddenly rivaled peak-season August numbers. Their experience highlighted one of many shifts in the evolving COVID-19 economy. Locally sourced foods—especially staple items—had gained a particular advantage, as grocery stores struggled to meet increased demand with goods from megasuppliers.

Craig wished a similar fate to local fishing families, but his training as an economist told him the odds were stacked against them. First came the bleak outlook for consumer demand. As the economic effects of mitigation cascaded across the nation, would there even be a near-term national market for lobsters? "The trouble is," said Craig, "that lobster is a celebration food out of state. And if people can't get together, if they're not on a cruise, if they're not at resorts or going to a nice restaurant, all the places where people splurge on lobster, if that's not happening across the entire world, you wonder about what the demand is going to be."

Then came the question of how long fishermen could wait out a freefall in demand. It was a sticky issue—complicated by the fact that Maine's lobstering industry is built on family ownership. Rooted in the state's "one license per captain per boat" rule, lobster-fishing families are product-generating islands. Family members often work together, rely on one another, and pour everything they have, and more, into their operations. That's where debt proves pivotal. "If you have a fisherman who has very low debt levels," Craig posited, "I think they can survive lower prices for a year or two. There'll be hardship, but they're not looking at bankruptcy." The real trouble would come with the far more typical scenario: "the state-of-the-art type operation where there could be hundreds of thousands in debt." Indeed, in recent years, as the industry had reaped strong gains, more and more lobster fishermen had leveraged themselves with high-cost investments in "new gear and new boats, often as a way to minimize their tax exposure during all these good years." Those fishermen "need to be bringing in three to five hundred thousand a year gross" to meet debt payments and keep their businesses going. "And if prices collapse," Craig added, "which they easily could, those fishermen face financial ruin."

Even with the promise of federal aid, prospects were bleak. In the first round of COVID-19 relief packages, Congress approved $300 million in relief for the entire U.S. fishing industry. The funds were split proportionally across thirty-one states— leaving just $20 million in aid to Maine. Fishermen immediately threw up their hands at the amount and pushed for more. Indeed, lobstermen worried that, even if the funding were to be increased, there'd be no guarantee that families like the Holts would benefit. They hadn't qualified for most of the early rounds of COVID-19 government relief. They'd gotten some Paycheck Protection Program funds to help their wharf workers, whom the Holts had kept on payroll, but beyond that, Mckenna and her family would have to turn to their savings if the fishing season went bust.

"You can't win with any situation right now," reflected Mckenna. "You need to go to work, but you ain't gonna make anything if you do, so there's no sense to go." Fishermen like the Holts, who were savers, could afford to wait—so long as things opened eventually. But for spenders—the ones who blew their summer and fall fishing cash "throughout the months that they weren't fishing," the situation would soon be dire. "They're trying to get their boats in and get going," said Mckenna, "when everyone else is pretty much just telling them no."

It was June, and the Downeast fishermen were still waiting. Despite signs that things were opening up in Maine, Mckenna didn't know when she'd get her traps in—or if she'd get them in at all that summer. "There's not even a price right now for the soft-shells I catch up in the river. You can't even sell them." If the wharf-based company Mckenna typically sold to were to start taking her soft-shells, it would have to give her three or four dollars a pound just to make it worth her while to fish. Meanwhile, down at the wharf, Mckenna's dad and brother wouldn't fare much better with their hard-shell lobsters, which typically fetched higher prices than the soft-shells. "Right now, they'd get two dollars a pound if they were to sell their lobsters there, when normally they'd be getting seven or eight a pound. You can't operate on just two dollars a pound."

Like the Marshalls, Mckenna's dad and brother had instead resorted to taking their lobsters and peddling them. "Dad goes to Waterville, and Matthew's in Bangor right now," said Mckenna. "Matthew's even gone and talked to a bunch of restaurants, because they're starting to reopen. But it's been a long, long drug-out process." By selling retail out of their trucks, Jake and Matthew were able to pull in six or seven dollars a pound, which at least allowed them to turn a small profit. "They try and keep the price as fair as possible," Mckenna said. "And they're selling enough—at least for now." As summer approached, the industry as a whole got a glimmer of helpful news: in response to lobbying by Maine's congressional delegation, the White House extended eligibility to lobster fisheries for funds from the Department of Agriculture's $30 billion COVID-response farm bailout. It wasn't entirely clear how much of that would flow to Maine's lobstermen, or exactly when it might arrive, but officials and the fishing industry cheered it as a step in the right direction.

As for Mckenna, she was more interested in fishing than bailouts—and was willing to "just hold off and wait a little longer," even as she held out hope that she might be able to set her traps by sometime in July. If she could do that, she'd have an outside shot at ending up with half or three quarters of what she would have made by fishing a full season. She was more than willing to put in the extra work, and fall had always been her strongest fishing season. She figured it might likely be so again—so long as the virus didn't come roaring back.

Chapter 22

Anchored

Across the river and around the bend of Downeast's rocky shores, Audrey's family faced similar worries. Audrey's dad and two brothers had fished through the winter. Their lobster yield, along with the prices it fetched, had made the off-season reasonably profitable. Now, they sat at home and waited for their state to reawaken. Augusta was abuzz with stern language, warning Mainers not to return too quickly to their work and life routines. Audrey knew the Bartons were fortunate to have the cushion of their winter fishing yield. There was no telling yet how things would unfold, and once they did, how far beyond the strictures of their homebound lives she and her family might be allowed to roam. One thing Audrey knew: she would almost certainly not be summer fishing. For the first time ever, she wished this weren't the case. Normalcy, here and elsewhere, was phantom.

Audrey sat in Grandma Sarah's house and wondered what lay ahead. The place was silent, save for the patter of Audrey's footsteps as she crossed the small, dark kitchen where Sarah had once held court. Audrey missed her grandmother. Sarah had been strong-willed and plainspoken. She didn't mince words and she didn't hold back. Even in the fragile years before she passed, she'd cut a lean and striking figure.

A few months earlier, Grandma Sarah had sat in that very room and reminisced about her childhood, as Audrey and Suzanne asked her to retell the stories they'd each heard dozens of times. Sarah, oxygen tank perched beside her, didn't need much encouragement—although she warned she wouldn't spill all her secrets. The best were being saved, she said, for her book, a tribute to the life she'd lived and the town she'd known as a girl—which unfortunately she was never able to complete.

Sarah had lived on the Back Bay Road nearly all her years. She'd watched her children and grandchildren and great-grandchildren grow up around her, and she'd helped them build their lives. When Sarah was in her prime, people said she could be a bit imposing, particularly when she was up on a horse—which was often. Indeed, she was an expert horsewoman, and a fine barrel racer.

Sarah's father had been a farmer. He'd hauled neighbors' wood. He'd broken their horses and worked their land. In due course, he'd seen an opportunity in buying and selling horses. He'd travel the state and bring them home, and Sarah would try them out until her father could find a buyer for them. "I got throwed a lot," Sarah recalled, but over time, her stubbornness outlasted that of the horses. Years later, she raised her two daughters—Audrey's aunts—to cherish horses nearly as much as she did. When her girls were young, Sarah decided it was time for them to start competing, and together they traveled as far as Texas to barrel race. Sarah liked to win, and she and her daughters often did. Along the way, they got to see a bit of life beyond the Back Bay Road. Sarah figured that didn't hurt them, and she had an openness about her that allowed her to make friends pretty much wherever she took the girls. Still, Sarah never got the itch to move away.

"I'd had opportunities," she remembered, "back when I was in high school. I had a chance to go to school in Utah and live on a ranch. And another chance, later, to stay with one of the stable people in Orono where my father did business and go to college in Bangor. Then, and later on, after we'd had the girls, I didn't want to leave home. Why would I? I was comfortable here. I had everything I needed or wanted."

When Sarah turned eighteen, she married a boy she'd known since elementary school, and together they built a solid life for themselves and their three children. After their children had children of their own, Sarah taught her granddaughters to ride and compete as soon as they were old enough. All the Barton girls did well under Grandma Sarah's firm tutelage. But Audrey, the youngest, stood out among them, as a quick study and a talent.

As the years passed, Sarah's age and illnesses bound her increasingly to her home. When the time came that she could no longer ride, she'd watch from her window as her daughters and granddaughters exercised their horses on the wide field that stretched to Audrey's house and tumbled down toward the bay beyond it. In late winter, at eighty-three, Sarah bid her family, and her horses, goodbye.

Six weeks later, Audrey returned to her grandmother's house on the broad hill atop the Back Bay Road. She'd just cut short a Florida vacation with friends, and like millions of Americans, she'd scrambled home amid the nation's heightening COVID-19 alerts. As Audrey traveled back to Maine, she and her parents agreed that she'd best go straight to Grandma Sarah's to wait out her fourteen-day self-isolation. From there, Audrey followed her social media as reactions to the virus unfolded among friends and family. The near absence of cases countywide hadn't made Downeasters more lax; if anything, it had made them more vigilant. Wariness mounted at "people not doing what they think they should be with social distancing." Some cursed the rising number of out-of-state plates. But for every angry post came tenfold offering help to neighbors needing food or provisions, praise for school-bus drivers delivering meals to kids, and cheers for the preponderance of local nurses and aides who worked in area hospitals and nursing homes.

There was fear, too, for the Downeast kids whose home lives were shaky even before Maine's shutdown—the 30 percent in Washington County who lived in poverty, the ones whose parents couldn't kick a drug habit, and the victims of household abuse. These children now sat in homes beset by anxiety. With grandparents, friends, and neighbors shuttered in their own homes, who would hear their cries? Many would struggle to keep their learning going. Some, lacking internet access, wouldn't have the means to try. School for them had been a safe haven, and teachers, their protectors. This too was gone.

Audrey's heart ached for these kids. She'd seen firsthand the burdens they carried to school each day. Each Friday since September, she'd returned home to volunteer at Milbridge Elementary School, the place she'd spent her earliest learning years. There, three of five students lived in poverty. Nearly a quarter of them qualified for special education services, well above the national rate. And 20 percent, the sons and daughters of migrant and immigrant laborers, worked hard to overcome barriers of language and culture.

Audrey had found her way back to her elementary school through Molly Richardson, a family friend and fellow Milbridge native who'd been pushing for years to make Washington County schools more "trauma sensitive." It was an idea that had come late to the area, more than a dozen years after inner-city schools across the nation had embraced it.

In the early 2000s, urban educators had zeroed in on the day-to-day stress that kids in tough circumstances faced, and had launched a move to combat the effects of home-based trauma in large-scale school systems. Relationships and trust building were at the center of their efforts. With the right interventions, they learned, kids could overcome the chaos in their homes and possibly improve their life chances. This was the work that Molly, a former Narraguagus English teacher and guidance counselor, was now introducing to Downeast Washington County, and that Audrey was witnessing firsthand by volunteering at Milbridge Elementary.

Five feet two, with a Diet Coke permanently fixed in her hand, Molly was a twelfth-generation Mainer, and one of a long line of Milbridge Richardsons. She graduated at the top of her class from Narraguagus High, was named valedictorian at Colby College, and had her pick of far-flung post-college opportunities. She resisted their lure and returned home. The decision suited her. In 2007, she was named Maine Teacher of the Year—the first to hail from Washington County in twenty-five years.

And yet, by her own account, she was struggling. "I had amazing students. We had amazing teachers. It wasn't about being a failing school or failing community. Something else was missing."

That something was a disconnect between what many of her students faced at home and what they felt they could reveal at school. "We're told growing up," said Molly, "that you can't bring your problems to work with you. The truth is you can't leave that stuff behind." With nearly "every student who walked through my guidance door at Narraguagus, it was all about trauma, poverty, and home circumstances that were shaping everything about where their future could go."

Molly wanted to do better. She'd heard about a talk being given in an eastern Maine town that's remote even by Milbridge's standards. On her way, she kept thinking, *Why am I driving all this way? What's out here?*

Once there, she knew. She watched, transfixed, as a graying, bearded man offered what, to Molly, was a radical way to think about Washington County's most at-risk kids. Working with researchers from Colby College and UMO, he'd hit upon the idea of using brain science to understand and address what was driving the academic and behavioral difficulties of so many local students. He named his program TREE, for Transforming Rural Experience in Education, and began searching for a team to pilot it. At the end of the talk, Molly told him, "I'm in." Within six months, he had tapped her to lead the effort.

Audrey had been eager to join as well. As she worked with Milbridge's kids, she began to see the difference she could make. Throughout fall 2019, she read with the kids, played with them, and guided them through assignments. Most of all, she showed them she cared. It didn't take much, this gift of encouragement—and it came naturally to Audrey. As she spent her Fridays with these kids, she realized the magnitude of what she'd grown up taking for granted.

The cross-generation connection between Molly and Audrey, exemplified in their work, embodies the promise that had flowed through previous generations of Downeast girls. These women, and others like them, are the glue that holds their hometowns together, women who, by virtue of their decisions to support

each other and to not leave, evince courage and faith in the dura-
bility of these beautiful places.

In late November, her weekend fishing duties done for the
year, Audrey also began coaching basketball for the town's four-
and five-year-olds. Though deeply rooted to her Back Bay Road
home, she found herself increasingly connected to Milbridge.
It was around that time, too, that Audrey broke up with Jack.
The relationship's end—although something of a bombshell
to friends and family, who'd long anticipated the pair would
marry—wasn't a surprise to either of them. Audrey and Jack had
talked about breaking up months earlier, when Jack had moved
to Machias to work as a barber alongside his father. But they'd
invested so much in each other, and they loved each other in
the vague way that often comes with extended courtship—so
they resolved to give it one more try. In the end, though, they
knew the relationship wasn't meant to be, and they went their
separate ways. There was no bitterness in it, only an absence of
mutuality.

Now that Audrey wasn't shuttling back and forth to Machias,
she had plenty of time to spare. She still had a handful of classes
to complete before her spring graduation, but none of it was terribly taxing. These days, she spent at least as much time at home
as on campus.

Mostly, Audrey was anticipating the coming fall with excitement. She'd gotten word that UMO had accepted her into the
graduate program of her choice and had awarded her one of
the most sought-after scholarships on campus. It came with full
tuition for her first year and summer of coursework, and more
than likely for her second and final year too. A free graduate
education would go a long way, especially now that Downeast's
lobster-fishing industry had been wounded.

As Audrey contemplated her future, she imagined a life familiar to what she'd always known. "My pull would be toward Downeast," she said, "and Milbridge has a special place in my heart. If I find a job nearby, if I can continue to help out at the elementary school and do my part in my community, I would choose that." Audrey couldn't imagine settling in another area, and "certainly not much farther from home than Bangor," unless perhaps she met someone who lived in another part of Maine. "But," she added, "my parents own the land all around my house, the land where my grandmother's house sits." When, in the past, Audrey's parents had discussed what might happen to Grandma Sarah's house, they'd turned to Audrey and said, "That house will be yours someday." And though it was bittersweet for Audrey to think of it, she knew that such a path, for her, would be just fine.

Chapter 23

Found

Before I'd spent time in Downeast Washington County, I had been told that I'd find tough circumstances there. The data had forewarned me, and depictions of challenges at every turn, relayed by people who'd lived in the region, had brought that struggle to life. I'd thought, once I was there, that I'd see the rural America that many of us originally from urban areas had come to expect: towns frayed by loss and abandonment; patchworks of economic blight, physical isolation, and social deterioration. And I found these elements too.

But beneath the weight of shared troubles, I found something else—the energy of shared community, helping ease burdens in ways that well-meaning strangers and codified institutions could never do. I watched and listened and partook. I developed friendships that have enriched me in untold ways. And along the way, I realized that what I was witnessing was the glow of what some might think was a lost America. It wasn't perfect. Far from it. In some ways, it was particular to place. But in the most meaningful of ways, this glow was rooted in people's outlook and choices rather than their economic circumstances or demography. The girls found strength and hope in their connection to others, and in the natural bounty that surrounded them. Each of their families, in turn, relied on fragments of that bounty, whether through fishing, farming, building, or simply serving their neighbors. Together, they carved a communion with the land and sea around them, and it sustained them. They built a foundation on perseverance and optimism—knowing that family and neighbors would be there to catch them if they fell, and to help lift them higher if their ambitions so led them. They protected one another in the face of threat or danger. When they encountered barbs, of which there were plenty, they banded together and dulled them. Their resilience was captured in the ephemerality of the phrase locals used to describe the difficulties that too many of them persistently faced: "hard times." Not poverty or destitution, but a headwind to withstand until they came out the other side. As if to say "this too shall pass," and with collective strength it can be overcome.

These were the ideals that cradled them from birth. This was the brickwork that allowed them to trust that what they had would outlast, and transcend, the opulence of far more "fortunate" communities. These Downeast towns, and others like them, would never be rich. They would not shine from the glitter of material gains. But should an economic downturn in those other places wrestle that glitter from those who lived and died by it, Downeast, at its core, would be no poorer in senses that mattered. Its people would understand what it takes to survive, because survival had long been the source of their sustenance. Its families would band together, not in self-congratulatory lip service to community, but in the barely perceptible heartbeat of service to others. At the end of each weary day, they would rest, knowing that their currency was their trust in the permanence of timeless ideals: a healthy fealty to nature's rule, an undying connection to the people they loved, the dignity of cracked hands and muddied shoes, and a self-sufficiency that had been woven into their beings as tightly as Grandma Sarah's canvas horse blanket.

This, then, was Sarah Barton's America—but it was Audrey Barton's America too. It was Josie's, Vivian's, Mckenna's—and even Willow's—America.

I'd been fortunate enough to meet Sarah and be in the room when she was reminiscing about her childhood with Audrey and her family. Sarah hadn't had faith that her beloved community would persevere. She'd believed that it had been surrendered to what she loathingly called "progress." Progress, to her, was anything that marred the simplicity of her childhood, or impeded "the whole neighborhood being like one big family." "Of course," she'd observed, with a wry smile, "we were all related. But I didn't realize that when I was young. We were, all of us, in and out of each other's houses and everybody else's, and we were outdoors all the time. And we used our imagination." When she wasn't outside playing, Sarah was working. She'd reminded Audrey of this as she'd absentmindedly smoothed the creases from her pristine kitchen tablecloth. "I started working when I was around twelve. I used to go in sometimes and work as a chambermaid with my mom, or take her place while she was sick or couldn't get there. I washed dishes for their dining room. We worked a lot as kids, but it didn't do us any harm. And it taught us a lot."

Years later, all too suddenly, it seemed to Sarah, things began to change. The difference hit her most when new technologies— wrapped in smartphones and tablets—found their way to the reaches of her beloved Back Bay Road. Then too, the old haunts in town began to close. The local hotel, the movie theater, the ever-reliable variety store. Routine errands that had been a bike ride away suddenly required journeys across highways. And while to many elsewhere in America, the world seemed to shrink with each iteration of innovation, the Downeast Sarah knew and loved seemed, to her, to grow more distant. She worried for her grandchildren and great-grandchildren. And she grieved for the existence modernity had stolen from them.

Yet, I think that what Sarah failed to see was that progress had not penetrated Downeast's soul. It had reshaped the contours of her hometown, perhaps, but the intergenerational ties that had bridged Sarah's family and extended to neighbors remained as strong as ever.

What's more, Sarah's Downeast had been enhanced by the arrival of newcomers from other regions—international and domestic. Farmworker and immigrant families had found in Milbridge a place for their children to thrive and contribute well beyond the blueberry fields and wreath factories in which they toiled. Their work ethic, ambition, faith, and unassailable familial ties helped them break down barriers. Most arrivals found, in Downeast, a community that welcomed and encouraged them, and they, in turn, excelled and embraced their new hometown.

Alexandra Alvarez and her family stand as shining examples. As young girls, she and her four sisters followed their parents and brother Downeast to work beside them in the blueberry barrens at harvest time. When Alexandra arrived, she hadn't seen her mother in two years. When her parents, who'd bounced between Florida and Michigan for seasonal work, landed steady jobs in a local sea cucumber factory, they decided to stay and raise their children in Milbridge. But soon after, the factory closed down. In response, Alexandra's parents dug deep into their entrepreneurial spirit and opened a small restaurant featuring food from their homeland. Today, Alvarez Mexican Takeout draws restaurant-goers from as far away as Portland—and locals regularly line up for food outside the modest structure. Alexandra excelled throughout her school career, graduated with honors from Narraguagus, and studied education at UMM. For years, she's dedicated herself to helping other farmworker and immigrant families through Mano en Mano, a local advocacy and support organization. She serves on the board of a well-known local women's health nonprofit, and is seen by many as a rising local star. Married, with a child of her own now, and continuing to live in Milbridge surrounded by her parents and siblings, Alexandra knows this is *her* community, the place she will always call home.

And Alexandra's story does not stand alone. As foreign-born and American-born newcomers alike have brought new energy and a distinct perspective Downeast, their sons and daughters have emerged as successful entrepreneurs, educators, and community leaders. The full value of their contributions is yet to be seen.

As for Sarah, while she had recognized and appreciated these and other changes around her, she had not fully grasped their value to the place she loved. Understandably (given her vantage point), she had not reconciled the essential truth that progress matters, in ways big and small, to Downeast's survival. Indeed, the region needs more of it. COVID-19 highlighted the painful reality of Downeast's limited access to broadband, negatively impacting kids' ability to study remotely, a reality in much of rural America.

And the paucity of modern health-care facilities has proven especially acute. Washington County's only two hospitals faced financial struggles before the onset of the virus; one had declared bankruptcy. Maine's two-month prohibition on elective medical procedures—coupled, ironically, with the virtual absence of COVID-19 patients in the state's rural areas—threatened to push these hospitals to the brink. Health-care staff were furloughed, already scarce services were reduced, and a population that is among the unhealthiest in the state was placed in greater jeopardy.

But innovation has found its way to key aspects of Downeast's economy, particularly in the critical area of commercial fishing. Downeast natives like Lauren Donovan, Olivia Marshall, Molly Richardson, and Craig Palmer—and nonnatives who chose to settle there, like Britt Frances, Ann-Marie Whalen, and Manny and Lois Parsons—have brought their own brands of innovation to those whose lives they touch. Their form of "progress" is tangible and meaningful, perhaps more so than in other places because it is infused with Downeast sensibility—informed pragmatism coupled with an undying loyalty to family and community. And so, to the extent that·innovation *has* altered central aspects of Downeasters' daily life, it has not overtaken them. The vast majority here remain far less fettered to material and technological pursuits than their counterparts in urban and suburban America. The routines of their waking hours, the time spent on lobster boats, the interconnectedness with neighbors, and the reverence for simplicity and minimalism has kept a strong hold on the residents of these tiny enclaves, etched in the edges of America's eastern coast.

There is resonance, too, in the central roles that women here occupy, and the culture of strength they embody. Downeast women wear the label of "fierceness" with pride. They emphasize the importance of resilience and stoicism to their daughters.

They nurture their girls' femininity—in this sense, most consider themselves traditionalists—while instilling in them the purest form of "feminism": independence, self-reliance, and an abiding faith in their ability to keep up with the men around them. Indeed, they are proof that feminism comes in many forms, and need not be so labeled to be real.

In the end, Grandma Sarah was at peace with herself—and with all that her Downeast had allowed her to build. She was grateful, too, for this seemingly unforgiving terrain had bestowed upon her all she needed, and more. She built a legacy from it that would long outlast her physical presence. And what she may not have realized—or perhaps she did: it is *this* legacy, along with the legacy of others around her who drew strength from being of this place, that continues to thrive in the girls whose lives are recounted in this book. Their journeys have only begun. Their life stories will not replicate Sarah's. They will not rest, as she did, on memories of untethered simplicity. Some will stay, and others will depart, perhaps, at some point, never to physically return. But even if they do not end up *in* the Downeast of their growing years, they will always be of it. Its robust heart will beat within them.

Epilogue

As I write, America, and the world, face profound uncertainty and loss. In the spring of 2020, the spread of COVID-19 left millions of Americans isolating themselves in their homes. And waiting. Like them, I thought constantly about my family and friends. About our future. Who, and what, collectively, would we have lost when this nightmare finally ended?

Each day was a journey. Time simultaneously raced and crawled. We eagerly awaited, and concurrently dreaded, the daily news. We had never before spent so many hours tuning in to our state and national leaders, heeding the counsel of public health officials, and checking on loved ones.

At home, the fortunate had someone to embrace. They did so more purposefully, as if to compensate for the distances from everyone else they'd been forced to endure. Some were not so lucky. They were alone, or worse yet, left helpless to learn that someone they love was forever lost. I counted my blessings as I sat beside a loving husband and daughter, and texted with my sister for daily commiseration. I called my parents, who had been holed up for weeks in their New York City apartment. They told me they were doing fine. I called again two hours later. I thought about the next time I'd be able to see them, to hug my dad or hold my mother's hand.

Together, we mourn the losses that mount across our nation and the world, and the incalculable sacrifices that have been made. Americans everywhere have quickly learned to live with less, to be resourceful with what they have. The least fortunate among us have suffered disproportionately. They have been forced to do without.

I consider, too, the shift in outlook this crisis has prompted—the ways the experience of it has awakened more middle- and upper-class Americans to the lure of sparseness. In the earliest weeks of the pandemic's onslaught, city dwellers who were fortunate enough to have suburban and rural homes to escape to—or relatives generous enough to share their space—fled their apartments. Those who remained encountered a postapocalyptic hush that echoed through their streets. Each day, they peered from shuttered windows for signs of life below. Each dusk, as they caught sight of frontline workers heading home, they opened those windows to join in makeshift symphonies of gratitude.

Many who'd chosen density now longed for space. Some, who'd become accustomed to outsourcing many of their daily chores, learned the power of self-reliance. When fabricated diversions were forced to close, families turned to nature to nourish their bodies and settle their souls. As parents spent more time with their children, they rediscovered the wonder they'd felt when they first set eyes upon them. I grieve the fact that it took a treacherous virus—and the unintended consequences of its mitigation—to prompt these awakenings. If only we'd stumbled on them without calamity.

Epilogue

I've spent the past four years witnessing the power of community and connection in one small corner of America. I first saw as a paradox the juxtaposition between Downeast's physical isolation and persistent poverty, and the robust connectedness of its people to one another and to the region they call home. I no longer do. I've come to realize how their sense of community—in all its physical, spiritual, emotional, and intellectual manifestations—has sustained and even galvanized them, through the toughest of times. It's a phenomenon that's become increasingly difficult to find in vast swaths of urban and suburban America.

Today, the yearning for that sense of community is stronger than it's been in modern history. We feel the power of it as, by necessity, we turn our bodies inward. We self-isolate. We sidestep neighbors at grocery stores. We tighten our masks and learn to mark the measure of six feet. And yet, as we distance ourselves to ward off a cunning illness, we learn the value of connection that transcends physicality. It is something Downeasters, and millions of other small-town Americans, have practiced for generations. And in the end, we are left to consider that, perhaps, it is not they who have been left behind, but the rest of us.

Acknowledgments

I have been blessed with a life surrounded by extraordinary people. Each of them, by inspiring and supporting me, has helped make this book possible.

I am particularly indebted to the following:

The five remarkable young women featured in this book, for trusting me to tell their stories and for their openness and bravery in sharing their past, present, and hopes for the future. Their families, friends, teachers, coaches, mentors, and school and community leaders, who opened their doors and patiently educated me about the ways of Downeast Washington County. Their lives of purpose, resilience, and optimism exemplify the best in all of us.

Reverend Scott Planting, for pointing me Downeast and helping make my first connections there.

My agent, Bridget Matzie, for the vision and creativity that brought this project to life and the skill and acumen that made it whole. Basil Smikle, for introducing me to Bridget—and for many years of friendship.

My editor, Gail Winston, whose belief in the power of this story never wavered, for her editorial wisdom and enthusiasm.

Acknowledgments

Neil Rosini, Julia Rosner, and Hayley Salmon for their indispensable assistance.

Those who read at critical junctures: Steve McKibben, for his incisive edits, and for the wise counsel to keep reaching higher. Ann Marie Lipinski, whose recognition of the centrality of girls and women sharpened my focus. Ray Madoff, for long walks and lunches at Johnny's and pushing me to hone my thinking.

Friends and extended family members: Carole Asher and Colleen Rowley Tsao for being my anchors and lifting me up at every turn. Jennifer Rearden for countless check-ins and confidences. Shayne Gilbert, Kara Hughes, Veronica Kenny-Macpherson, Elise Kipness, David and Victoria MacDonald, Mitchell Moss, Silvio Nahum, Leon and Nadia Oxman, Kathy Piazza, Alexandra Stanton, Reverend Dr. Robert and Presvytera Nikki Stephanopoulos, Diane Oxman Wender, and Howard Wolfson—all of whom have helped ground and sustain me. The Georges, Polymenakos, Protonentis, and Vassilakos families, with whom I grew up, for wonderful memories and lively family gatherings.

My nieces and nephews, who bring joy to Margaux and her grateful parents. Katie, Christopher, and Charlie, for being outstanding role models and fort-builders, and for their ideas and encouragement throughout this process. Julia, Danielle, and Zoe, for making every visit and sleepover fun.

My brother Chris's many friends and mentors, who always remember. Among them: Michael Aaronson, Kate Boo, Jackie Calmes, Pam Abel Davis, Joel Getz, Kristin Goss, Jon Kaplan and Jill Wilkins, Alan Murray, John Schafer, Gene Sperling, Josh Steiner, and Amy Waldman. Above all, John and Rosalee Di-Iulio, who embraced me when life was most difficult and have guided and inspired me every day since.

Acknowledgments

My sister, Stephanie Georges, who personifies smarts and strength, for her keen insights and constant support on this work and well beyond it. Chris, our gentle knight, who left too soon, whose compassion and courage knew no bounds. Most of all, my parents, whose unwavering encouragement, wisdom, integrity—and love for each other and all of us—are my greatest inspiration. They are a daily reminder of all that is worth striving for in life.

Jeff, my beloved husband, for introducing me to Maine and wrapping your arms in mine. For your multiple, painstaking reads of my drafts and the genius of your edits, which made this book far better than it would have been. For sharing your beautiful heart and mind.

Margaux, our kind, spirited, and incomparable daughter. You are our morning light, our everything.

Notes

THE GEOGRAPHY

xiii downwind to go eastward: "Downeast or Down East Maine," Acadia Magic.com, https://acadiamagic.com/Downeast.html. Mainers use the terms "Downeast" and "Down East" interchangeably.

PROLOGUE

5 rates of opioid overdoses in the nation: R. L. Haffajee, L. A. Lin, and A. S. D. Bohnert, "Characteristics of US Counties with High Opioid Overdose Mortality and Low Capacity to Deliver Medications for Opioid Use Disorder," *JAMA Network Open* 2, no. 6 (2019):e196373, Figure 1. Opioid Overdose Death Rate per 100 000 People by US County, 2015–2017, https://jamanetwork.com/journals/jamanetworkopen/fullarticle /2736933.

7 recent female-authored, rural-focused memoirs and novels: See, for example, Sarah Smarsh, *Heartland: A Memoir of Working Hard and Being Broke in the Richest Country on Earth* (New York: Scribner, 2018) and Elizabeth Wetmore, *Valentine* (New York: HarperCollins, 2020).

CHAPTER 1: THE DOWNEAST LIFE

18 Nearly 30 percent of its kids: The Annie E. Casey Foundation, Kids Count Data Center (December 2019), "Children in Poverty in Washington County, 2015–17," https://datacenter.kidscount.org/data/tables /1562-children-in-poverty-2005–2018?loc=21&loct=5#detailed/5 /3298/false/37,871,870,573,869,36,868,867,133,38/any/11725,3331. Washington County also contains two of the state's five Native American

reservations. Although Washington County's Native population is not within the scope of this book, the challenges faced by the roughly 1,500 members of the Passamaquoddy tribe who inhabit the county's two reservations are significant—far more so than those faced by those outside the tribe. For example, childhood poverty across the two reservations averages close to 50 percent, average per capita income is less than $14,000 (roughly half that in the rest of the county), and life expectancy is far lower than in the rest of Maine. See U.S. Census Bureau, "American Community Survey 5-Year Estimates," Census Reporter Profiles for Passamaquoddy Indian Township Reservation and Pleasant Point Reservation, Washington County, ME, 2018, http://censusreporter.org/profiles/06000US2302957082-passamaquoddy -indian-township-reservation-washington-county-me/, https://census reporter.org/profiles/06000US2302957090-passamaquoddy-pleasant -point-reservation-washington-county-me/.

18 ranked as the least healthy: University of Wisconsin Population Health Institute. County Health Rankings & Roadmaps, Maine, 2020, "Overall Rank," Washington County, https://www.countyhealthrankings .org/app/maine/2020/rankings/washington/county/outcomes /overall/snapshot.

18 options for recovery: Market Decisions Research, Hart Consulting Inc., and the Maine Center for Disease Control and Prevention, *2016 Maine Shared Community Health Needs Assessment: Washington County*, November 3, 2015 (updated February 29, 2016), 21, https://www.maine .gov/dhhs/mecdc/phdata/SHNAPP/documents/county-reports /whole-reports/Maine%20Shared%20CHNA%20WASHINGTON %20County%20Report-2-29-16.pdf.

18 overall life expectancy: University of Wisconsin Population Health Institute, County Health Rankings & Roadmaps, Maine, 2020, "Life Expectancy," https://www.countyhealthrankings.org/app/maine/2020 /measure/outcomes/147/data?sort=sc-2.

19 more than one-billion-dollar statewide endeavor: This estimate, calculated in 2016, represents the "overall economic output of the wholesale lobster distribution network" in Maine, including both the retail value of lobster harvests (also commonly known as "lobster landings"), which in recent years has been between $450 million and $600 million annually, and the overall dollar value contribution of the lobster distribution supply chain to the Maine economy, which was calculated to be

Notes

approximately $1 billion annually. The supply chain includes the role dealers play in buying lobsters; grading them for quality and quantity; and packing, processing, and shipping them. The supply chain was also estimated to support roughly 5,500 jobs—in addition to the 6,000 or so commercial lobster fishermen who work along Maine's shores each year. Colby College professor of economics Michael Donihue for the Maine State Department of Marine Resources in Partnership with the Maine Lobster Dealers' Association, "Lobsters to Dollars: The Economic Impact of the Lobster Distribution Supply Chain in Maine," Final Report June 2018, 1–3, http://www.colby.edu/economics/lobsters/Lobsters2DollarsFinalReport.pdf.

19   at the bottom of Maine state rankings: Market Decisions Research, *2016 Maine Shared Community Health Needs Assessment*, 36.

CHAPTER 2: BEGINNINGS

26   highest rate of drug overdoses of any county in Maine: University of Wisconsin Population Health Institute, County Health Rankings & Roadmaps, Maine, 2020, "Drug Overdose Deaths, Number of Drug Poisoning Deaths per 100,000 population," https://www.countyhealth rankings.org/app/maine/2020/measure/factors/138/data?sort= desc-3.

27   number of drug-affected babies born: The Annie E. Casey Foundation, Kids Count Data Center, "Babies Born Exposed/Affected to Substances in Maine," 2019, https://datacenter.kidscount.org/data/tables/9828-babies-born-exposed-affected-to-substances#detailed/5/3284–3299/false/1729,37,871,870,573,869,36,868/any/19127,19128.

27   Maine's national overdose death rate ranking: Centers for Disease Control and Prevention, "2013–2017 Drug Overdose Death Rate Increases: Age-adjusted rate of drug overdose deaths by state—2013 and 2017," https://www.cdc.gov/drugoverdose/data/statedeaths/drug-over dose-death-rate-increase-2013-2017.html.

30   Blueberry Capital of the World: Cherryfield is home to two of the state's six major wild blueberry producers. A decade ago, the state of Maine supplied more than half of the wild blueberries consumed in the world. But the industry is now in decline. In 2012, Maine blueberries fetched 76 cents per pound. By 2016, the per-pound price had plummeted to 27 cents. Many of the area's smaller blueberry farms

have stopped operation altogether. The main culprits: overexpansion, resulting in a blueberry glut, and fierce competition from Canada, where government subsidies allow growers to underprice Maine producers.

CHAPTER 3: GIRLS GONE FISHING

34 from lobstering to quahogging: Quahogs are small, hard-shell clams that are harvested in Maine's coastal waters (but can also be found in coastal waters up and down the Eastern Seaboard) and are considered particularly good for chowder. Maine ocean quahogs, which have a distinct rich, reddish-brown color, are also known as mahogany clams. While harvesting of soft-shell clams is done by hand in the intertidal zone (the shore where land and sea meet between low and high tides), quahogging is primarily done in deeper subtidal waters, through the use of a small dredge that captures the clams from the ocean floor. According to the Maine Clammers Association, "historically, the bulk of ocean quahog fishing activity in Maine has taken place on two large quahog beds near the town of Addison and Great Wass Island—about a 60 square nautical mile radius" off the coast of Downeast Washington County. See "Shellfish," https://maineclammers.org/clamming/shellfish/.

38 one thousand hours of fishing: Maine's apprenticeship program offers students a path to earn a commercial lobster fishing license that avoids long waiting lists. The state's Department of Marine Resources requires apprenticeships to be sponsored by a commercial license holder, to fish for one thousand hours "over a minimum of 200 days stretched out over a minimum of two years" and to earn a high school degree or equivalent. When Mckenna started apprenticing, students had to meet these requirements by age eighteen; in 2016, the state raised the age to twenty. Without this program, young people would have to get on the end of a long line of aspiring commercial license holders. In 2018, there were nearly 250 names on the waiting list, which is spread across Maine's seven "lobster management" zones. And Mckenna's zone, which includes Washington and Hancock counties, generally holds the most names—in 2018 it had 54. Because those at the top of the list must wait for three fishermen in their fishing zone to retire before being granted a license, the wait time outside of the apprenticeship program often extends for years. For full regulations see: State of Maine, Department of Maine Resources, MRS Title 12, Chapter 619, Lobster

and Crab Fishing Licenses; State of Maine Department of Marine Resources, "Law Change Affects Eligibility Criteria for Maine Students Who Want to Start Lobstering," April 8, 2016, https://www.maine.gov /dmr/news-details.html?id=678715.

CHAPTER 13: ADRIFT

139 access to obstetrics and prenatal care: U.S. Department of Health and Human Services, Health Resources and Services Administration, Maternal and Child Health Bureau, "Rural and Urban Women," Women's Health USA 2013, Rockville, Maryland: U.S. Department of Health and Human Services, 2013, https://mchb.hrsa.gov/whusa13 /population-characteristics/p/rural-urban-women.html.

139 Medicaid and Medicare: American College of Obstetricians and Gynecologists, "Health Disparities in Rural Women," Committee Opinion No. 586, February 2014, https://www.acog.org/clinical/clinical-guidance /committee-opinion/articles/2014/02/health-disparities-in-rural -women#:~:text=ABSTRACT%3A%20Rural%20women%20 experience%20poorer,on%20the%20region%20and%20state.

139 "delayed care or no medical care": American College of Obstetricians and Gynecologists, "Health Disparities in Rural Women."

139 nurse shortage: Jackie Farwell, "Study: Maine's Going to Have to Find 3,200 New Nurses by 2025," *Bangor Daily News*, February 14, 2017, https://bangordailynews.com/2017/02/14/news/as-maines -population-ages-nursing-shortage-looms/#:~:text=Without%20 action%2C%20Maine%20will%20face,Maine%20System%20and%20 nursing%20organizations.

139 $49 million bond issue: Department of the Secretary of State of Maine, "2018 Maine Citizen's Guide to the Referendum Election," 2. Question 4 reads as follows: "Do you favor a $49,000,000 bond issue to be matched by at least $49,000,000 in private and public funds to modernize and improve the facilities and infrastructure of Maine's public universities in order to expand workforce development capacity and to attract and retain students to strengthen Maine's economy and future workforce?," https://www.maine.gov/sos/news/2018/citizens guide.html.

140 surplus of nurses by 2030: U.S. Department of Health and Human Services, Health Resources and Services Administration, National Center for Health Workforce Analysis, *National and Regional Supply and Demand Projections of the Nursing Workforce: 2014–2030*, 2017,

Rockville, Maryland, 10–11. https://bhw.hrsa.gov/sites/default/files/bhw/nchwa/projections/NCHWA_HRSA_Nursing_Report.pdf.

142 interpersonal violence: Market Decisions Research et al., *2016 Maine Shared Community Health Needs Assessment.*

CHAPTER 15: MONEYBALL

162 more than 80 percent support: Phi Delta Kappan, "The 49th Annual PDK Poll of the Public's Attitudes Toward the Public Schools" (Arlington, VA: Phi Delta Kappa International, September 2017), 4, https://pdkpoll.org/wp-content/uploads/2020/05/pdkpoll49_2017.pdf.

162 more participation barriers than cities: Lucinda Gray and Laura Lewis, *Career and Technical Education Programs in Public School Districts: 2016–17: First Look*, NCES 2018–028, April 2017, U.S. Department of Education, Washington, DC: National Center for Education Statistics, 1–2, https://nces.ed.gov/pubs2018/2018028.pdf. The nationally representative survey of school districts defines a CTE program as a "sequence of courses at the high school level that provides students with the academic and technical knowledge and skills needed to prepare for further education and careers in current or emerging professions." Districts "were instructed to include all CTE programs that the district offers to high school students, including programs provided by the district or by other entities (such as an area/regional CTE center, a consortium of districts, or a community or technical college)."

CHAPTER 17: POWERED BY LOBSTERS

175 20 percent higher than in 2018: Penelope Overton, "Though Maine's Lobster Harvest Was Smallest in 9 Years, Value Remained Steady," *Portland Press Herald*, March 6, 2020, https://www.pressherald.com/2020/03/06/lobster-harvest-smallest-in-9-years-but-value-increased/#:~:text=Updated%20March%206-,Though%20Maine's%20lobster%20harvest%20was%20smallest%20in%209%20years%2C%20value,lobster%20hauls%20back%20in%201880.

179 full-time captains: "Museum exhibit showcases women who lobster," *MaineBoats.com* (blog), July 17, 2019, https://maineboats.com/blog/2019/museum-exhibit-showcases-women-who-lobster.

CHAPTER 18: BEYOND THE SUNRISE TRAIL

187 weaker religious affiliations: Gallup recently found that roughly 40 percent of millennials are church members; when members of Gen-

eration X were their age, roughly 60 percent belonged to a church. See Jeffrey M. Jones, "U.S. Church Membership Down Sharply in Past Two Decades," Gallup.com, April 19, 2019, https://news.gallup.com/poll /248837/church-membership-down-sharply-past-two-decades.aspx.

187 30 percent of eighteen-to-twenty-nine-year-olds: Pew Center for Religion and Public Life, "2014 U.S. Religious Landscape Study," Pew Research Center, 2014, https://www.pewforum.org/religious-landscape -study/.

188 believe in God: Pew Center for Religion and Public Life, "2014 U.S. Religious Landscape Study." Fifty percent of respondents expressed "absolute" belief in God, 21 percent "fairly certain." Thirty-eight percent said religion is "very important," 29 percent "somewhat important." For all adults, 83 percent expressed absolute or fairly certain belief in God, 77 percent said religion is very or somewhat important.

188 millennials seem to have marched: Millennials are defined as those born between 1981 and 1996; Gen Zers as those born after 1996. Deckman, a political scientist, conducted research on Gen Z indicating there may be a leveling off in religious attitudes within this group. Deckman compared 2016 results about millennial attitudes toward religion with her own 2019 survey results of Gen Z, and concluded that "Gen Z Americans look awfully similar to their Millennial elders when it comes to religious affiliation and religious behavior." Melissa Deckman, "Generation Z and Religion: What New Data Show," *Religion in Public* (blog), February 10, 2020, https://religioninpublic.blog/2020/02/10/generation -z-and-religion-what-new-data-show/.

188 nearly twenty-year-old Gallup study: When comparing similar age groups, Gallup found religiosity to be consistently highest in rural areas. Lynda Lyons, "Age, Religiosity, and Rural America," Gallup.com, March 11, 2003, https://news.gallup.com/poll/7960/age-religiosity -rural-america.aspx.

188 similarly sparse "amenity rich" areas: Michele Dillon and Megan Henley, "Religion, Politics, and the Environment in Rural America," Carsey Institute, University of New Hampshire, Issue Brief No. 3, Fall 2008, 2, https://scholars.unh.edu/cgi/viewcontent.cgi?article=1046 &context=carsey.

CHAPTER 19: SOMETHING BETTER
200 average age of first-time mothers: Quoctrung Bui and Claire Cain Miller, "The Age That Women Have Babies: How a Gap Divides

America," *New York Times*, August 4, 2018, https://www.nytimes.com /interactive/2018/08/04/upshot/up-birth-age-gap.html.

200 women without a college degree: One promising Washington County–based effort for low-income parents without a college degree is Family Futures Downeast (FFD). Launched in 2015, FFD is a two-generation program that gives low-income parents the opportunity, with multiple supports (including coaching, transportation, and technology resources), to attend the University of Maine at Machias or Washington County Community College, while providing their young children with on-campus early childhood education. The program, whose stated goal is to "reduce poverty, create employment opportunities and improve stability in Washington County families," is a collaborative of six organizations and agencies. See https://familyfuturesdowneast.org.

200 53 percent of Washington County's births: "Washington County, Maine Demographics Data," Population Charts, Towncharts.com, 2018, https://www.towncharts.com/Maine/Demographics/Washington -County-ME-Demographics-data.html.

200 within one point of Mississippi: "Percentage of Births to Unmarried Mothers by States," Centers for Disease Control and Prevention, National Center for Birth Statistics, 2018, https://www.cdc.gov/nchs /pressroom/sosmap/unmarried/unmarried.htm.

201 poverty rate for children who lived in single-parent households: "Child Poverty in America 2017: National Analysis," Children's Defense Fund, September 12, 2018, 3, https://www.childrensdefense .org/wp-content/uploads/2018/09/Child-Poverty-in-America-2017 -National-Fact-Sheet.pdf.

201 less likely to complete school: See Robert I. Lerman, Joseph Price, and W. Bradford Wilcox, "Family Structure and Economic Success Across the Life Course," *Marriage & Family Review* 53, no 8 (2017): 744–58, DOI: 10.1080/01494929.2017.1316810; Sara McLanahan, Laura Tach, and Daniel Schneider, "The Causal Effects of Father Absence," *Annual Review of Sociology* 39, no. 1 (2013): 399–427; Adam Thomas and Isabel Sawhill, "For Richer or for Poorer: Marriage as an Antipoverty Strategy," *Journal of Policy Analysis and Management* 21, no. 4 (2002): 587–99. In recent years, arguments have flared over the relationship between single motherhood and poverty, and there has been significant policy debate over how to address it. The purpose of citing research around single parenthood and child poverty is not to wade into the policy debate, but to highlight that the struggles of low-income sin-

gle mothers in Washington County, Maine, and elsewhere—and the impact of those struggles on their children—are real, and should not be overlooked. Indeed, this reality underscores a central point in this book: the importance of local community, extended family, teachers, and mentors in helping at-risk children combat and overcome the hurdles they encounter.

205 more likely to want to stay: Pew Center for Religion and Public Life, "What Unites and Divides Urban, Suburban, and Rural Communities," Pew Research Center, May 22, 2018, https://www.pewsocialtrends.org/2018/05/22/what-unites-and-divides-urban-suburban-and-rural-communities/.

205 know all or most of their neighbors: Pew Center for Religion and Public Life, "What Unites and Divides Urban, Suburban, and Rural Communities." See also National Public Radio, the Robert Wood Johnson Foundation, and the Harvard T. H. Chan School of Public Health, "Life in Rural America," October 2018, 6–7. This nationally representative survey of rural adults found that "rural Americans identify close-knit communities and social connections as major strengths," and that "a significant share of rural Americans are optimistic about their lives."

205 Their attachment is fostered: Robert A. Petrin, Kai A. Schafft, and Judith L. Meece, "Educational Sorting and Residential Aspirations Among Rural High School Students," *American Educational Research Journal* 51, no. 2 (2014): 294–326. The study used national data and focus groups to counter a prominent "brain drain" argument that rural adults in schools and among family and community members "play an unwitting role in their own decline" by encouraging them to leave. (For more on this argument, see Patrick J. Carr and Maria J. Kefalas, *Hollowing Out the Middle: The Rural Brain Drain and What It Means for America* (Boston: Beacon Press, 2009). Petrin et al. determined that most rural educators are not, in fact, grooming high-achieving students to leave; rather "contact with teachers and other school personnel about career or future plans tends, if anything, to be associated with student aspirations to remain in rural communities. In this sense, the data points to rural schools as "potential drivers of economic development" by encouraging students to stay and engaging with local employers to connect them to students. Finally, to the extent that leaving was encouraged by schools, family, and community, it "was perhaps paradoxically seen as an important means of achieving community revitalization and

sustainability," bolstered by expectations that leavers would ultimately return.

206 challenges of internet access and transportation: Pew Center for Religion and Public Life, "What Unites and Divides Urban, Suburban, and Rural Communities." "Prime-age workers" are defined as twenty-five-to-fifty-four-year-olds.

206 something different seems to be happening: Journalist and *Heartland* author Sarah Smarsh recently made the case for "the less common narrative" that more Americans are seeking out "less bustling spaces"— either as returners to their hometowns, or as newcomers. See "Something Special Has Happened in Rural America," *New York Times*, September 17, 2019, https://www.nytimes.com/2019/09/17/opinion/rural-america.html.

CHAPTER 21: FIGHTING BACK

213 Maine's confirmed case count: Indeed, by the end of August 2020, after state officials expressed much concern that an influx of summer tourists would prompt a COVID-19 spike (and put measures in place to restrict entry from some states and regions), Maine recorded a total of 4,082 confirmed cases, with 418 hospitalizations and 132 deaths. Totals for the state's three most rural counties—Lincoln, Piscataquis, and Washington—stood at 52 confirmed cases, with just 4 hospitalizations and 1 death. "COVID-19: Maine Data," Maine Department of Health and Human Services, Maine.gov, https://www.maine.gov/dhhs/mecdc/infectious-disease/epi/airborne/coronavirus/data.shtml.

213 cargo planes in Canada: Steve McKinley, "Reverberations from COVID-19 reach Canada's East Coast—and Its Lobster Fishery," *The Star*, February 25, 2020, https://www.thestar.com/news/canada/2020/02/25/lobster-price-drops-as-coronavirus-chokes-chinese-market.html. Over the course of 2018 and 2019, the U.S. government imposed tariffs on various categories of goods from China. China retaliated with tariffs on a range of U.S. goods, including a 25 percent tariff on lobster (raised to 35 percent in 2019). China's action all but eliminated its market for lobsters from Maine—cutting Maine's exports of lobster to China by 50 percent. Canada, which remained outside the tariff war, became the beneficiary of Maine's lost China sales. Yet, as a June 2020 Quartz media analysis noted, "the industry managed to pivot," finding markets elsewhere, including "processed products, from canned lobster to pet food, that could still find year-round US

demand." In the end, despite the effect of tariffs, gross dollar sales remained near record highs, and well above those realized earlier in the decade. David Yanofsky and Tim McDonnell, "Trump Wants to Save the Lobster Industry, After Boiling It Alive," Quartz, qz.com, June 25, 2020, https://qz.com/1873487/trump-is-bailing-out-maines-lobster -industry-from-his-trade-war/.

214 filed for unemployment: Peter McGuire, "New Jobless Claims Surged by 16,000 Last Week as More Workers Qualified for Benefits," *Portland Press Herald*, May 7, 2020, https://www.pressherald.com/2020 /05/07/jobless-claims-surge-to-16000-last-week-as-more-mainers -become-eligible-for-benefits/.

215 "the most economically vulnerable" state: "Ranking States by Coronavirus Structural Vulnerabilities," Oxford Economics, Global Macro Service Research Briefing, https://www.oxfordeconomics.com/my-oxford/publications/551704.

220 a step in the right direction: Laurie Valigra, "Trump Memo on Lobster Aid Leaves Industry Wondering What's Next," *Bangor Daily News*, July 5, 2020, https://bangordailynews.com/2020/07/05/business /trump-memo-on-lobster-aid-leaves-industry-wondering-whats -next/.

CHAPTER 22: ANCHORED

227 large-scale school systems: The effort's roots go back to a 1990s landmark study conducted by Kaiser Permanente and the Centers for Disease Control. Researchers discovered links between extreme stress in developing brains and production of the hormone cortisol. Excessive cortisol eats away at response controls, ultimately triggering a near-constant fight-or-flight mode. It also induces anxiety, depression, sleeplessness, and lack of focus. See V. J. Felitti et al, "Relationship of Childhood Abuse and Household Dysfunction to Many of the Leading Causes of Death in Adults: The Adverse Childhood Experiences (ACE) Study," *American Journal of Preventive Medicine* 14, no. 4 (1998): 245–58, https://doi.org/10.1016/S0749–3797(98)00017–8.

CHAPTER 23: FOUND

236 hospitals to the brink: Spencer Roberts, "Lost Revenue Significant Problem for Rural Hospitals," WABI-Maine, April 30, 2020, https:// www.wabi.tv/content/news/Lost-revenue-significant-problem-for -rural-hospitals-570085031.html.

Index

Index

Index

Index

Index

Index

Index

About the Author

GIGI GEORGES, Ph.D., has had an extensive career in politics, public service, and academia. A former White House special assistant to the president and communications director for the New York City Department of Education, she has taught political science at Boston College and served as program director for the Harvard Kennedy School's Innovation Strategies Initiative. She and her family live in New Hampshire and Downeast Maine.